WHEN IS YOUR TIME UP?

STEPHEN PAUL TOLMIE

authorHOUSE·

AuthorHouse™
1663 Liberty Drive
Bloomington, IN 47403
www.authorhouse.com
Phone: 833-262-8899

Published by AuthorHouse 07/25/2020

ISBN: 978-1-7283-6767-5 (sc)
ISBN: 978-1-7283-6876-4 (e)

DEDICATION

I dedicate this book to my mother, Nellie Irene Tolmie. She always gave me her love, her understanding, her comfort and her compassion. I am who I am, what I am and what I may yet become, due to her support and guidance. To this end, I have written a poem for my mother, as an indication, of what she has been to me, in my life.

A Mother's Love

Mother's love is given, in great quantities
There is no height, not depth to it;
Nor width, nor length you see.
There is no beginning, nor no end.
A mother gives and gives some more, through all eternity.

As her store of love is deep—as deep as the sea.
She is always ready to give her love, her time and energy.
She is never unapproachable and always,
The first one on the scene.

So to you, my Mother I give a slight bit of me;
Not in the same proportions; but still enough indeed.
I can never repay you, for your love, time and energy.
But in some small way, I hope to say
my love forever, I give to thee.

You have always been there for me;
There is nothing more I need.
As I write this poem for you.
Always know, you will be in my heart, with me
from now through all eternity.

Your Loving son.....Stephen Paul Tolmie.....July 7th, 2005

ACKNOWLEDGEMENT

I have a very special friend, Eileen Fralick who was willing to look at my finished book. She was willing to make suggestions, offer her opinion and just an overall good look, at this book, for its content.

With the pandemic (coronavirus in 2020) that was in existence at the time of this book, there was no way to get together, for this to be accomplished.

Once again, Eileen, I appreciate your willingness, to be of assistance, if the possibility presented itself. Had not the covid-19 been in existence, which affected all our lives and living style, this would have been accomplished.

Stephen Paul Tolmie

IN APPRECIATION

I wish to extend, a special thank you, to a special friend....Yoram Snir. He has extensive knowledge of design, along with computer skills and artistic talent, all which are very evident, in the book covered he created.

Again, I am very fortunate to have his friendship, his time he freely gives, and his talent, for producing, this special book cover design.

Again, this was the finishing "touch" that was required to bring my book to life!

Stephen Paul Tolmie

PROLOGUE

Before, we get started into my book, which is an examination of many aspects of and including near death experiences, coming back from death, and grieving death of a loved one. The preparation for your death, how to organize your estate, and arranging for an executor of your estate. These are just a few topics, under review throughout this book.

We first should examine, what our life involved, what has happened in our lives, and what are the expectations, that come with our death. Also, the effects of our death on the people we left behind? What was the outcome felt by them, with our death? What effect did it possibly have on their lives?

We are really here, for a very short period of time, be it lengthy or short period of years. We have gathered our wealth, tried to look after our health, but really, the important thing in our lives, is our SPIRIT! What will become of it? We spend very little of our precious time, even contemplating the hereafter, and what is to become of our SPIRIT SOULS?

The important issue, is to live your present life, the best way you can, being kind, thoughtful and of a good heart. This time has been allotted to you, by a HIGHER POWER! Be all you can be, and be all you should be, and place no thoughts on "TOMORROW"!

Your NUMBER may come up? Without warning, all that you have done in that time frame has been recorded, and examined with your death. A very befitting verse, found in the Holy Bible, fits in very well with my introduction, and is known as Psalm 23.

The Lord is My Shepherd

The Lord is my shepherd; I shall not want
He maketh me to lie down in green pastures:
he leadeth me beside still waters.

He restoreth my soul: he leadeth me in the path
of righteousness for his name's sake.

Yea, though I walk through the valley of the shadow of death, I will fear
no evil: for thou art with me; thy rod and thy staff they comfort me.

Thou preparest a table before me in the presence of mine enemies:
thou anointest my head with oil; my cup runneth over.

Surely goodness and mercy shall follow me all the days of my
life: and I shall dwell in the house of the Lord forever.

THE WORD OF GOD!!!

WHEN IS YOUR TIME UP?

I am a firm believer, that when you were born, you're given a NUMBER, on your descent to earth, and this number, when it is finally called, you have no choice in the matter. OR DO YOU? I mean, that even though your expiration number has finally arrived, some outside circumstances may alter your fate. Maybe, some divine intervention has come your way, to assist you with your final outcome? This possibly, was a gift to avoid death, at this time? Then, giving you time, to reassess your actions and your purpose here on earth?

Death is called a "great equalizer" for a reason-- the rules are the same for everyone. Well, almost everyone! As I have just indicated in my thought process, some humans seem almost un-killable. Either via extreme luck, tenacity or a freak of biology, these people survive almost lethal situations. There will be more reflections on this subject, which people have had, in escaping their deaths.

What REALLY is your life's purpose? It may be as simple, as getting up and making your decisions of that day's activities. Possibly, if you got up on the wrong side of the bed, your behaviour for that day can shape your mood and actions, the day may consist of. If on the other hand, you wake up rested and ready to start your day, this too can shape what your day may entail. You then, set your goals, aspirations or direction you will be taking for that day. This also, outlines, what you hope to accomplish in that day, and therefore, you have created meaning and direction, in your new day.

In essence, your life's purpose can be summarized, as "living each day, as though it could be your last day, here on earth!" You should never lose sight of this fact that you're living, for the here and now. Don't worry about the end of your life? When it may come? Life is about leaving a footprint of yourself, through what you did on earth, and with your time here. You want to be remembered for the kind, considerate and loving things; you contributed, when you were alive. This is your lasting legacy that you were here. That you also contributed, to making a better life, for those you came into contact with. Been remembered, for those deeds, are the mark of living a successful life; which each of us should strive for.

Summarizing: the purpose of living is to give, "Your Life Meaning", knowing that you were here; that you left your mark! You came to this earth as a baby; grew to a teenager; then to adulthood, and left impressions of your life lived, all along the way, in your life!

All of this contributes to the purpose and meaning of our lives. What we want to do with our lives and contributions we hope to deliver. We hope to develop our goals and our expectations for our lives. We take the values we respect, and we impose standards onto ourselves. WE also try to determine the right and wrong of our personal goals. This then is the total package, giving us true meaning to our lives. By leading by our own example, through life's passage ways; the end result is what gave meaning, and purpose, of our lives lived. Don't always try to second guess yourself; by constantly looking for alternative answers, which we came up with, as our first choice. We shouldn't be looking harder for a second or third angle? When you stop to use logic and common sense, that we all possess, we are staring at the right answer, we first came up with.

THE TREE OF LIFE

The tree of life is so like man, ever stretching to the skies
Its branches ever reaching upward, as though to heaven above
Like man's quest here on earth, to reach for that high unknown
The tree requires the stables of life, for its very existence here
But man in his slight wisdom, knows these details all too clear
The tree roots, securely planted, are not allowed to roam
But man's feet here on earth, have mobility all their own
Unlike the tree, man does possess, a single separate entity
A brain you see, though seldom used, a total shame indeed
The tree of life depends on man, for its daily life's survival
Man depends on his own life's skills, to hopefully see his tomorrow
Which is a sad virtue, for his thinking process, is not always clear
He makes good and bad decisions, its effects are not yet known
Man should take his life's lessons, from the tree of life pursuit
As our single life's purpose, to reach for heaven above
As the tree stretches forth its limbs, ever skyward in its growth
We should heed this very lesson and praise the Lord above
For all HE has done for mankind and this our earth as well

Author: Stephen Paul Tolmie

In writing THE TREE OF LIFE poem, I thought, how very simply it applied to mankind. How he/she should relate these thoughts on life, to their own personal life experiences. One should take a moment, to ponder the logic, and its impact on their lives and well- being. In digesting, these very words, you soon realize a sense of worth, from these words. Also, how it may or may not impact on you? Hopefully, some value and a somewhat new prospective meaning, in your life are realized? Then take it a step further, as to how it applies in your everyday life.

Well, we all need a reason to wake up, as previously mentioned, to start another day in our lives. Possibly, from this poem that was given for your consideration, it may even put a step in your walk, a smile on your face, and the realization that life is not all bad! IT's" TRULY" WORTH LIVING!

So in simplicity: THE TREE OF LIFE poem, with its applied logic, can be summarized this way:

Live simply, love generously
Care deeply, and speak kindly
Live your life to the fullest
Be happy within yourself
Take time to smile with yourself and others
Life is rich and full, you only get one chance

Author: Stephen Paul Tolmie

WHAT IS THE TRUE MEANING OF LIFE?

It is a simple, but yet a difficult question to answer; in just a word or a small phrase, for its apparent transparency. We could ask ourselves questions like:

"Why are we here?"
"What is life all about?"
"What is the purpose to my existence?"
"Where do I go from here?"
"When do I start my pathway to life?"
"What direction is my life destined to follow?"
"Who is my guide in this life?"
"Is life all about religious practices?"

These are just a few of the questions, which may appear, in your mind to ponder? Is" Happiness" my primary quest in my Life Purpose? All seem very logical, and a reasonable conclusion to come up with; but is there truly a bigger picture? Maybe, the securing of goods, good health, and knowledge of what makes us tick in this world, will define us? Possibly the correct pathway, which will lead us, to enrichment of our life, which we constantly seek, is what we should follow?

Yet, as I alluded to, the bigger picture may very well be; the ultimate good that mankind does, in his time here on earth; for a Higher Power to evaluate. What has he/she given to others and left this earth a better place? A place where he/she left their footprint for others to remember what they did? What did they in fact accomplish? Often, people are seeking their purpose, their goals, and their very reason for existence! They are constantly searching, be it through religion; through research at a library, through meditation, or even through experimental drugs. They are all striving for the same end result, their expectation, they will achieve! Do they select going down one set path in life, or do they choose the other path, and just go along with what they were told? What is the real truth, or not? Then not to question, the reasoning and logic, as to what they have been told? All too often, they are no further ahead than when they began. Now, do they accept this fact in life, or choose to do harm to themselves? The result, they may end up in their minds state, only having their body in this world, their mind not of this world?

This is becoming quite the topic for exploration, and I really wish to go down another road, in my examination. What is the purpose of your existence here on earth? Why do we wish to be here? Why do we fight to actually stay here? This then, is the end result; we are all seeking, and is the title of the book. "WHEN IS YOUR TIME UP?

There are a few examples of people, who been confronted with a situation; that might very well have cost them their lives, and instead cheated death! Only to still be alive, and been able to tell of their close encounter, with the "Angel of Death"!

DEATH is called the great equalizer for a reason—the rules are the same for everyone. WELL ALMOST EVERYONE! AS we discussed previously, some rare humans seem to be almost un-killable. Either extreme luck, tenacity or some freak of their biology, these people survive almost lethal situations.

There was a man, who while checking on the water pressure in his apartment; after the Public Utilities, had done some alterations, to the entire system. He decided to check the toilet pressure by flushing it. He, not knowingly; had giving it a slight tap, leading to the toilet blasting, into tiny porcelain shards. This caused him to be wounded and needing stitches. He was in the right position, in the bathroom, not to have received a fatal injury. HIS NUMBER WASN'T UP?

Another instance, when a man was trimming branches off his tree, with his chainsaw. He slipped and fell onto the chainsaw, slicing through a portion of his neck. He cut through several blood vessels, severing them from their normal position, and even included his jugular vein. He was very fortunate; he missed his carotid artery, an injury, with instant death.

Was this just "Pure Luck" that was on his side? Was it possibly a "Guardian Angel" looking after his well-being?

Or, is this simply explained, as HIS NUMBER WASN'T UP? Another situation, where a woman, while skiing; tumbled into a mostly frozen lake, and ended up trapped under the ice. When rescuers discovered her; she had been under the water for over an hour, and had no pulse. The medic team began to warm up her blood, and to everyone shock, her heart started beating again. She was still able to go on with her life. Was this DEVINE Interaction? Was it merely HER NUMBER WASN'T UP?

I heard of a story of a railroad worker, falling off a moving train, and lost half his body. When the train finally came to a halt, his entire lower half was still trapped, under the wheels. Again, what presence was with him in his hour of need? Giving him the ability to remain conscious, and calmly calling 911 for help? I believe again, the presence of a Guardian Angel was with him, and saw that HIS NUMBER WASN'T UP?

Then, there was the story of a guy, just sitting on his porch, when he heard a loud LOOK OUT! He had just enough time, to see that his roommate; had dropped a 50 pound air conditioner, directly above his head. He had instantly leaned forward, but still the air conditioner, brushed over his back of his neck. He still had to go to the hospital for a bruised spine and a total physical; to be sure there was no other damage to his body. Was this just his Good Reflexes? Was his Guardian Angel watching over him? Was HIS NUMBER NOT UP? This is something to think about, in this near death experience!

There is an incident, where a person almost drowned while white water rafting. This person started to panic, which is a normal reaction; when he realized, he was stuck in the rapids. There was a raft and four other people on top of him, and they weren't moving. At this point, this person just gave up, and eventually started to black out. This person's world seemed to get quiet and peaceful. When he was almost completely out; someone jumped into the water, and pulled him out from under the raft. Was this a Coincidence? Was this just Good Luck? Was his time here on earth not yet up? Again the big question "Why was he saved"? Was HIS NUMBER NOT UP?

There is a story, of a man driving his car out in the country, and passing nothing but open farm land. Out of the corner of his eye, he spotted something moving, and running straight in his direction. Suddenly, he realized it was a big deer, and it didn't appear to be stopping in its tracks. It jumped straight into my car directions. I attempted to swerve to avoid hitting the deer, but it struck the back portion of my car; and then continued on into more traffic. When, I had swerved to my left, I was right in front of a car heading in my direction. My quick reflects kicked in, and I swerved to the right, back into my own lane. I then, just drove off, like the whole ordeal, never even took place. In a few brief seconds later, I realized that I could have been killed. It hit me just like a panic attack, my heart was pounding rapidly; my body began to shake and the sweat poured down my face. I totally, realized that I had a close encounter with the "Angel of Death", but fortunately MY NUMBER WASN'T UP?

I recall an incident, where a small boy, fell into the ten foot deep end of a swimming pool. Either, to his young age; or not mature enough to know what was happening, he was later asked of his ordeal. He explained that he felt really peaceful, and didn't truly understand what was happening to him? He said that he wasn't scared. Just before he blacked out, his brother pulled him out of the water, and into safety. Fortunately, his brother, or a Guardian Angel was watching over him, to ensure the proper action was taken! This near death experience, ended thankfully, in a continued life for this young lad and to the full life that was intended for him. Again, was this his Guardian Angel "stepping in or some "Higher Power"? WAS HIS NUMBER NOT UP?

Finally, my last example, of a near death experience was this incident.

A man was climbing a rock face and suddenly slipped some thirty to forty feet down. He didn't see any place to grab onto, to momentarily save himself. The man, just accepted his fate that he was going to die, as it was two hundred feet, to the bottom. He never believed, in the story, that you see your life flash before your eyes, but it "Truly Does Happen"! You seem at this very moment relaxed and time slows down; seemly to a crawl, and that's what probably saved my life, been calm and relaxed. Likely, I wouldn't have had the faculties, to catch a ledge, that was my life saver!

Again, did Someone Intervene? Was it just this man's quick reaction time that saved him? Was it not his time to die? WAS HIS NUMBER NOT UP? This gives me thought to ponder, in the fact that you truly have a number. When it is up, there still may be a way to elude the final fate, which was approaching? Still, I wonder if there isn't a "Guardian Angel" that is truly looking after you, or truly a "Higher Power"; over seeing Your Time of Life on Earth!

I would, now like to reflect, on this author's close call with DEATH, from his childhood to adult life. There are several examples, which do exist, for your insight into my life.

My first example would have been in my childhood, at Long Point Beach, where my grandparents had a cottage. My sister was a good swimmer and I unfortunately was not. It's not surprising, one summer day; while at the beach, she beckoned me to join her out in the lake. I was hesitant at first, as it looked further out, than I felt comfortable with. She still kept saying; that there was sand bars along the way, for me to rest, on my journey out to her. So, off I went, and indeed I found a sand bar, on my first attempt to go out to her. After a little rest and reinforcement, that I could indeed do this venture, off I went in her direction. When I was almost to my sister, I again got tired, and went to put my feet on the ground, but there was none to be found. Instantly, I started to flounder and thrash in the water, as the panic took hold! Something, inside my brain told me to get a grip on myself; think about my situation, and how to resolve my problem? I started to dog paddle towards my sister, and upon reaching her; I knew I was safe to put my feet down. I was both terribly afraid but also relived; that I had thought through the process, and not drown. To this very day, deep water and I are not good acquaintances; but much respect on my part, for the water and the situation it can produce. MY NUMBER WASN'T UP?

My second close call came, in my teenage years, when I was involved with the Scouting. My mother, been a leader of what is known as a cub troop (kids 8 to 12 years approximately) and I had moved up to the next level of scouts (kids 13 to 17 years of age approximately). My mother and other leaders, would during the summer months, take these kids to a camp. This was for a week of activities, crafts, obtaining badges and just generally a fun week. This occasion, the theme entailed Indian crafts, stories and Indian games. On the wrap up of the week's activities, the parents arrived to pick up their kids; enjoy a camp fire and singing the songs their kids, had learned through the week. I was assigned the job of lighting the camp fire and had been given the Indian name which represented "God of Fire". I was on top of the hill, with my torch and coal oil, in preparation of been called upon. I wanted to be sure, that the torch would light, so I kept dunking the torch into the coal oil. I didn't realize, in the dark, that the coal oil was running down my clothing. When the Indian "God of Fire" was eventually called upon, to come and light the fire; I struck the match to the torch and I instantly "Became a Human Torch". I still wanted to do my duty, of starting the camp fire. I ran down the hill, jumped over some people in the process; stuck the torch in the campfire, and then jumped into the creek, to extinguish myself. It would be a huge understatement, to say that I didn't make a "Grand Entrance"! I also made a very lasting impression! The people at the campfire were in shock! I had severe burns, only to my hands thank God! The good thing that came out of it; I didn't have to help pack up all the camping gear, and general cleanup of the grounds. This was a courtesy, for the next group of people who would be using the facilities next week. This property was owned by the "Scouting" organization, for all members, to have at their disposal. I was very lucky that only my hands had been burned. It appeared initially, with all the flames of fire on my body; a different result would have been the case. Was someone of 'Great Divine" looking after me and had seen MY NUMBER WASN'T UP?

My next experience, with" death", came as a young adult of nineteen years of age. I had gotten my driver's license at sixteen; and was able to purchaser off my father, his trade in vehicle. I felt, like I was on top of the world; for in my mind state, I had obtained it all!

I was going to spend New Year's Eve with my girlfriend, who was babysitting a neighbouring child. I thought it best to do a test run; to see where the location, for my night's journey was located. I then picked up the girlfriend, and proceeded with her directions, down the road. I was glad I had asked for this test run, as it involved many up and down hillside roads. I was really starting to think, that this property was never going to be located? It was in the winter months obviously; as I came over the top of one hill, on my descent downwards. I could plainly see a pickup truck, parked sideways on the roadway. His vehicle had been abandoned; the driver was seeking help, I assume, when I appeared at the scene. Because, I was young and lack mature thinking, I didn't want to hit this vehicle. I was thinking my car insurance would sky rocket? I decided to put my car into the ditch, as my only possible solution. Well, the ditch turned out to be a 40 foot drop over the hillside. My little brain was still thinking I could steer around this big maple tree, which was heading in my direction. HOW ABSURD!

The impact, of the car hitting the tree; then falling to the ground and catching immediately on fire, was the direct result of this ordeal. The girlfriend had been thrown out through the windshield and I had ridden the car to the bottom. On impact, hitting my head, breaking my ribs and receiving several cuts to my body. I was now totally unconscious!

Waking up, seeing the car on fire and feeling trapped; I kicked out the window, to escape the car. My first reaction (strange as it was) was the car been on fire; that I needed to extinguish it. I started throwing snow on my car, totally ignoring my hurting body. How strange the thinking process, or lack of it, at this moment? But in reality, the car was totaled and of no value. Checking on the girlfriend and me should have been the number one priority? Upon, reconnecting with the girlfriend, I discovered all she received from the car accident; was a cut on the head. I was in fact, the only one really hurt! We had to walk a couple of miles for help, and the people we found drove me to the hospital. They then called my parents. A hospital stay was the order of the day! Drinking ginger ale in the hospital was not what I had planned to do? I had bigger plans in mind, to bring in the New Year, as a celebration of its arrival!

When, I finally got out of the hospital, I had a broken nose, two black eyes, broken ribs and a "hell of a headache". I asked to go by the gas station, where my wrecked vehicle was located. Upon, walking around the car, I overheard a man say; "I bet they died in the vehicle" and a small smirk, crossed over my lips. Again, the good Lord was looking after me. MY NUMBER WASN'T UP? I was to live another day, and hopefully, a wiser young man from this experience?

The next close call, I had in my adult years, was also in a car crash. This was totally unexpected? It was while driving at night, as I was going down a county road, on my way to see a friend. I had decided to get off the main highway and take a short cut, by heading across the county road. I was driving on a gravel road and doing the posted speed limit.

This roadway also had small hills to go up and down. I thought there wouldn't be much traffic on this roadway; and so I didn't have the inclination to slow down, when approaching these hills. Also, added to this fact; I hadn't seen a single car, since I originally started to use this roadway. Coming up one of these hills; I was confronted with bright headlights in the middle of the road, as I descended down the hill. I couldn't figure out for the life of me, why this vehicle was in the middle of the road? I thought that either this vehicle would turn off its bright lights, as a courtesy or law requirement; to dim the lights, but this wasn't the case. As I said, I hadn't slowed down, but was still doing the posted speed. I thought any moment; the car would at least get to the side of the road? This didn't happen either? I realized I had to make a decision. I opted to put the car in the ditch, rather than hitting the car head on. Because of my speed and the ditch been quite deep; I flew out of the ditch midair and flew over an object, and ended up in another ditch. Then, I again flew out of that one; as well, and ended up sandwiched, between two huge maple trees. In a split second, it seemed I was knocked out, having hit my steering wheel. Coming too momentarily, I realized, the whole front end of my "Ford Explorer Sport SUV", was now sitting, on the inside of my car. Some of the windows were smashed, and the air was filled; with the smell of oil and gas, as I sat there; surveying my surroundings. I realized I had to get out of the car. I pulled myself through the window and hit the ground. I was still a little shaking up, as the car was off the ground a few feet in the air. The driver, of the other vehicle, was now walking towards me. He wasn't sure I had lived through this ordeal? He then asked me, if I was OK.

I touched my head and felt no blood, and was reassured, that indeed I was alive; with a huge headache. I asked the man, what the HELL he was doing in the middle of the road, with his bright headlights on. He replied he was backing up his black trailer (with no visible lights on it) into his driveway. He exclaimed, he didn't think anybody would be using the road at this time of night. He was taking his time, to make sure he lined up his trailer, totally with his driveway. He had no awareness of any approaching vehicles. The police came and decided it wasn't anybody's fault, strictly wrong place; and wrong time, sort of thing, for the both of us. I thought this was very strange, as nothing had happened to his truck or trailer? My vehicle was totalled! I guess I was left to carry, the total expense all on my own? In retro-specs, I guess, I should have been grateful, that I was still alive, without too much harm to my body. My thoughts however, were on the money it would cost me to replace my vehicle. Again, what I should have been thinking; and thanking GOD that HE was there to look after this poor soul; in my hour of need. I should have also, been thankful that MY NUMBER WASN'T UP? I was to live another day and to continue on my life's journey.

This poor author has had a slip of memory, and forgotten another close call with death, when I was quite young. It was in the winter time, and as we lived close, to Port Stanley (Lake Erie) my parents, sister and I, went for a drive down to the lake. We were eager, to see what winter wonderland was on the lake. My sister, and I asked, if we could go out and play on the ice hills, which had formed out on the lake. We had come up with the idea, to play "hide and seek" with one another.

AS children, you don't think of danger; strictly the fun aspect of running up and down the ice hills, and trying hard, not to be discovered by our siblings.

It was on one of these occurrences, that I came down one of these ice hills; and hit a soft spot in the ice, then falling through. For a few seconds, I didn't realize what had just happened? Then reality took hold, and I realized what had just happened? Fortunately, the water level was not to the top of the ice, or I would not be here today. There were a few inches, of distance between the water and the ice. I could, also see blue sky, above the ice surface, where I was trapped. Where I existed, was very dark, and the coldness of the water started to register on my body. You don't apparently come straight back up, but shoot up on an angle; then the fear factor, started to register on me. I had no idea where the hole opening was, and PANIC started to enter my brain. I got a grip on myself, and started the thought process of looking for the hole. I started, first feeling my way along the ice in one direction, then turning around, and going back in another direction. I must have had my Guardian Angel there with me; sent by the Lord, to assist me with my escape. I located the hole, with the fresh air on my face feeling great. I tried pulling, as hard as I could; to pull myself up out of the hole, but there wasn't anything to grab onto? I continued falling back into the hole. My sister was yelling my name, and I was able to hold onto the top of the ice hole, to respond to her. She also, must have had some Divine Guidance from above; as she pulled off her scarf and throw it in my direction. I was able to grab hold of it, and between her pulling, and me thrusting my body upwards; I finally had success, and was out of the ice hole, FREE ONCE AGAIN! The long journey to the car, my frigid body, and clothing seemed to be restricting my movements. I had the strong willed desire within me; to reach the car, and its safety, which drove me onwards. Upon, reaching the car and the instant feeling of the warmth of the interior; was like winning a huge prize. My parents were instantly in shocked of my ordeal; as they had to cut and rip my clothing, from my body. They wrapped a blanket around me and headed for home. I had pneumonia, from this near death experience, but it was a very close call! A Near Death Experience!

Had I not stopped my panicking, understanding my situation; how to resolve it, and how to escape, I would have died. Added to this, was my sister arrival, to assist in pulling me out. All these factors, I feel where not of my own doing? A Divine Interaction, as the Lord, again said MY

NUMBER WASN'T UP? The Lord said, "Stop with my Stupidity" and to live a full life! Thankful Once Again!

As you can see, this author, has had a few close encounters with death, and has survived, to live another day. I believe, I have survived, due to Divine Intervention, My Own Wit and a Strong Belief, in the fact of a Number, been given you at your birth. All these factors come into play! Your death will not happen, till this number does in fact come up! Then, there is no recourse, but to meet the fate, that has come your way.

Not everyone believes as I do, but there ARE some, who think as I do. That possibly, you had a near death experience; miraculously come back from death, and possibly, other factors were intervening for you. Stories about people dying, and coming back to life; grab our attention in a way, which few other things do. Possibly, a lot of it has to do with what people see, in their near death experiences? Even when people's bodies or brains have technically shut down; those who are then resuscitated, still frequently report having an experience. They report everything, from complete emptiness; to vivid visions and sensory experiences.

Where your thoughts fall after reading this, can depend on whether your religious/spiritual upbringing, plays a big part in your belief. Or, as to whether you're a non-believer, and chose to use logic and common sense, in your analogy. Possibly, it could involve using all of these, in you're trying to understand the unknown? After all, your belief system shapes how you can view and process the world. Is a near death experience, from a technical standpoint, or your body reacting to trauma? Your belief systems, might then, also shape how you perceive the experience itself? It is very possible, that some people believe that there is just emptiness, where they are trapped. In their mind's state; a large void of total unawareness and a very bleak dark hollowness exists.

There are others like myself, who think of it as a state of total peace; of happiness and a state of enlightenment. Here, we are reconnected to the loved ones, which were taken from us earlier. This is my hope that I wish to experience from my death and it's not like if I don't like the experience

"I can say stop the train and let me off"! I would rather live my life, in hope of what is to come; rather than fear of the unknown and, what is to come from that experience.

I guess the Big Sixty Four Dollar Question is: "Is there life after death; or is there just blackness, to greet us when we die?"

The answer to that question depends very much, on your upbringing and religious attitude. But still, no one has a firm answer, one way or another, to this question? There are those, who have died on the operating table; or come close to death, and then made it back to our world. Their experiences are the best account, we have of what's waiting for us; after "the Act of Living is Done" and the curtain comes down, as the "Act of Life is Over"!

What happens after we die? Many of us wonder what happens after we die. We lived before we came to earth, and we will continue to live after we die. Having this "Faith" both provides comfort, and peace about death. While, we mourn, for those loved ones we've lost, there is hope—Death Is Not The End!

When we die, our spirit and body separate. Even though our body dies, our spirit—which is the essence of who we are—lives on. Our SPIRIT goes to the spirit world. This is a waiting period, until we receive the gift of resurrection; when our spirit will unite with our bodies. The resurrected body cannot die, and will be perfect---free from pain, sickness and imperfections. As a believer in God, I think everyone, who has faith, will be resurrected.

There is a story, of a man who died in a car accident, and was later revived. He said, as he was waiting for the ambulance to show up, a woman came to him and stayed. She told him everything would be okay and she would be there, as long as he needed her. He stated, that he felt this immense calm and peace, as this woman, made him warm and comfortable. There was no woman present, and he was totally unconscious, during this whole time period. They revived him at the hospital, and he still kept looking for this mysterious woman.

Was this a Guardian Angel? Was this just a Higher Power, which put into his mind; the calm and peaceful mood, while he waited, to return to his body? HIS NUMBER WASN'T UP?

Another incident, when a daughter and mother were in a bad car accident. The mother went into cardiac arrest, and was resuscitated with the paddles. The mother told the daughter, that she saw herself floating above her own body, and then ended up in a tunnel. She said she suddenly heard her deceased uncle's voices; telling her to go back and, that it wasn't her time yet! After hearing this comment, from her uncle; she said the tunnel sectioned off, and she went down that fork, ending up back into her own body.

This story enforces my theory, that you are given a NUMBER at birth, and if that number hasn't come up; you may very well escape the 'Angel of Death". Also, that a "Higher Power" had interceded in this woman's fate! HER NUMBER WASN'T UP?

Another, interesting story, is of a man feeling that he was in a deep blackness, like in a deep sleep. One moment, you're going about your life, and the next thing you know; you wake up in a hospital room, four days later. The doctor tells you suffered a case of ventricular fibrillation. He said you were on the floor; without a pulse, for about ten minutes, before been zapped twice; to bring you back to life. Again, HIS NUMBER WASN'T UP? Again, fear or anxiety didn't exist, in his recollection of this experience. It felt like a deep sleep, peace and calm, while waiting, to return to life. Had this major decision, been made on his behalf, by a "Higher Power"; gives one time to pause, to think and be thankful. Another incident, of a man going into ventricular fibrillation; then cardiac arrest, as the man was on a gurney, in the emergency room. From his account, time had just faded away and shifted to crimson/black nothingness. I went from feeling; I was going to explode, to utterly feeling tranquility. I felt myself retuning, back once again to my world. He described this experience, as though coming out of a long tunnel. At a frightening huge speed! After, having this body sensation, I passed out, and woke up three days later, in the intensive care unit.

Coming back from death, appeared to take its own sweet time, but he did return to live on. HIS NUMBER WASN'T UP? His calling to meet his maker had not been scheduled!

There is another story, of a lady's experience, after been away overdose, on her lithium. She stated that she woke up in a field with her grandparents around her. There was a ball of light, like the sun, that spoke to her, which she interpreted as God. She was told that she could stay there is the afterlife; or she could go back, and have to deal with the consequences, of lithium poisoning in her body. This condition would cause her immune system to be pretty weak; along with her thyroid, but she chose to come back, and then woke up.

This story is interesting, as it instills my belief; that we will be reconnected, with our deceased loved one, and where we could spend eternity. Although, this lady chose to come back to life; even with the problems she would face, life was still pretty special to her. This to me, enforces the belief, that because she was allowed to choose, HER NUMBER WASN'T UP?

There is a story of a young man, after a serious accident; feeling like he was lying in a tube. He didn't know where he was or what had happened to him? He felt restricted in movement, and a few seconds later, he felt the life flow out his arms and legs. It was though; somebody was disconnecting every part of my body! Just before, I lost consciousness; I remembered hearing people's voices, shouting medical terms. He also heard his father's voice, crying for help, to save his son's life.

After that scene, I had a moment of darkness and rest. Everything was gone! The only thing I remember is waking up; to a doctor's voice which felt like an eternity later.

Although, this young man had no recollections of bright colours, tunnels or people waiting to greet him; still it shows the Higher Power, listening at a father's plea; to not take his son. This young man was way too young and should have some time on earth as HIS NUMBER WASN'T UP?

Lastly, a story of a mother, having major health issues, of mild stroke and heart attacks. In order to fix up her heart, they had to literally stop her heart. This is her recollection of that experience. She said, she found herself in a place; that was somewhat cloudy/stormy sky, and the sun setting. She said, she was standing atop of a cliff face. She tried to walk to the edge, to get closer to the drop; but people wouldn't let her. These people were people she knew, like family, friends and people who previously died. She said all these people had something to say to her; though she wouldn't say what anyone had said. She stated an older version of my sister's child; wanted to play with her, and so she went along with it. As they played, the world around her, started to grow green, vibrant; the sun started to rise, and the storm was then swept away. After what seemed like a few hours, she was sent back to her body. HER NUMBER WASN'T UP?

Again, from this author's prospective; it instill that we WILL be reunited with loved ones, in the afterlife! Not all is bleak and black! It also instills in my mind; of peace, tranquility, happiness, and the reunion of departed loved ones. It also shows me, that the body spirit does leave our body; and as long as our NUMBER hasn't come up, we still remain on earth. If, on the other hand, our NUMBER has been called; that's when the transition does happen. It's something not to be feared, but looked forward to; for a union with loved ones, for all eternity.

HOW DO YOU FEEL NOW? Do any of these change your outlook of what to expect, when you die? I know it does for me! I have a thought, which is appropriate, at this moment to pass on, dealing with the topic of life and death.

> Life ends for everyone, when you stop dreaming
> Hope ends for everyone, when you stop believing
> Love ends, when you stop caring for other people
> Friendship ends, when you stop sharing with others

I hope, you feel as I do, that these simple statements, in reality encompass the whole meaning of life and our life's purpose here on earth. It does at least from my perspective; I feel this totally says it all!!!

HOPE WINS OVER FEAR.........every time!

When one's life is over, it's this transformation process; of leaving one's body behind and your body's spirit, proceeding on to the next journey. Wouldn't it be a great feeling, to be at total peace, and having this floating sensation? All the while, waiting the possibilities of seeing old relatives, friends and family, from your past existence on earth spirit reunited with my wife, my parents, grandparents and friends.

Couldn't this reuniting, with those you loved, be a glorious, accelerating and the happiest feeling you ever had? Not in your earthy body, but your SPIRITUAL BODY? Now to know that in eternity, you will exist with all those you cared for; never experiencing death, and the loss again of a loved one. Now through all eternity, with love and happiness, as an everyday experience forever.

Now as the author, I would like to tell you of the passing, of my beloved mother. I was sitting beside my mom in her hospital bed, while thinking of her love for me; her total attention to my needs, from birth to adult life. How it never wavered, not for a moment! My mother was my rock and refuse, and I was very blessed, to have such a wonderful mother. I was recalling my life, through my memories of her love; and kindness that she willingly gave me, throughout my life. I now looked over at her, in her bed, sound asleep. She had been in almost a comma state, for quite a period of time, and it was tearing me apart.

In a heartbeat, she raised her body from the bed, and looked at me in my chair. Her eyes weren't open, strictly two black holes in her head, was all I seen. After, a few brief seconds, she fell back onto the bed, and was now lost to my world.

In my heart, I would like to think that she wanted one last look at her son, before she passed. I would also like to think, that this hopefully, was a picture remembrance of me; to take with her, on her journey to heaven. To be united with all our past loved ones, who had preceded her!

At the time of her death, I didn't realize this at the time; but there was a feeling of "total peace and calm" in the room. There weren't any sounds, if so, they seem non-existent. The air had a heavy feeling and of utter stillness, expressing the momentary atmosphere.

I didn't see the "Angel of Death", but there was this feeling in my heart and brain; that something had lifted my mother's body upwards. I knew she had no strength. Her life's body had been lying with no motion, as none of her muscles; had been used in a long period of time. The pushing of her body upwards would have been impossible; it totally would have required assistance.

I would like to think, that the "Angel of Death", does possess the ability to have compassion; when this is the last moment, of a person's life, here on earth. Does he have a connection to the person who is dying? Possibly, he bequeaths the "dying person's last wish"? In this case, it was my mother's love for me and to have one last look at her son. This is totally my belief. I felt like I had received the greatest gift of all. I received a lasting memory, to carry me throughout my life time.

I had only wished that when my wife had passed, that I had been able to experience this unique feeling. There were too many nurses rushing around her and we were never alone.

This priceless gift, of a second of connection to each other; as she passed on, would leave this memory. This gift would carry me through my lifetime, without her. Now she was gone, my heart was shattered and my life with her is now a void. I would never experience life again with her, but I would have my loving memories, of this beautiful lady.

At this point, in our discussion of near death experiences and coming back from death; I would like to relate, a little of my insight, into this very subject. I had lost my wife, my companion, my soulmate, and my very rock of stability. I would like to share with you some poetry, which I wrote; to show my pain, my loss, and my despair. My world had now collapsed!

On the following pages, you will find four (4) poems I wrote, to help in the healing process. Hopefully, allowing you the reader, to reflect on your departed loved one. You might possibly, wished you had put pen to paper, to release your pain with their death? This would help with your inner emotion of loss; and now a life, without that special soulmate. This would be your connection, to that time of loss, and the heartfelt memories you shared.

IN MEMORY

AS you go through life's challenges
You'll have your ups and downs.
But when you find your soulmate
The challenges will quickly dissipate.
She is always there, to cheer you up
And intervene on your behalf.
She's there at the end of the day
To make your life's circle last.
A rare jewel, to say the least
She can always make you smile
And encourage you to do your best
This special lady, who was my life
Her memories still live on.
I cherish the time I had with her;
Time continues to move forward;
Life seems an endless flow.
Separation still exists between us;
My heart still does not glow.
But I knew the best is yet to come.
When once again reunited with her.
Life's circle will then be completed
A union of one to the other
for all eternity.

Author: Stephen Paul Tolmie

MY SPECIAL LADY

I constantly now miss you
If I could only find the way
as you made my life worth living
in a variety of different ways.
Your smile lightened up my world
and created, so many happy days.
Your very presence in my life
made life itself, seem all worthwhile.
For now I am without you
I have even lost my smile;
My life seems bleak and worthless.
There is no joy to life itself;
I merely go through the paces,
hoping you will return to me
to reunite us once again.
Then my life will be complete.
Happiness will enter in my world
I will always hold you tight
and live again, a happy man.

Author: Stephen Paul Tolmie

ONE LAST

One last moment together
One last spoken word
One last presence of you
One last tear or more
One last image to store
One last song to share
One last conscious moment
One last kiss….wanting more
One last love connection
One last moment of living life
One last moment of feeling whole
One last
One last and you slip away
Leaving a void
But lasting memories

Author: Stephen Paul Tolmie

MY LOVE IS FOREVER

I was once blessed with love
The feeling of closeness to you
You were my gift from God above
To have the whole day through
How now my life has changed
No longer safe in my arm
Your time has come to leave me
My sense of worth removed
The void of closeness to you
Now fills my world complete
I must now search my memories
For your love, I surely need
Rest now my love, my lady
As my love will never die
I know now, we will be together
We will always live forever
As our minds will be connected
Throughout all eternity

Author: Stephen Paul Tolmie

Now, let's take a look at the concept of a Guardian Angel, and explore what these two words actually mean?

Here are some thoughts, on what, it might mean possibly?

1. A Guardian Angel is a spirit, which is believed to watch over and protect a person.
2. A Guardian Angel is an angel, which is assigned to protect and guide a specific person.
3. A Guardian Angel is believed, to take care of a particular person.
4. A Guardian Angel serves to protect, whichever person God assigns them to.

There is also, the thought that a spirit is assigned to be your Guardian Angel, before you were even born. They are yours exclusively, like a nurturing mother; tending to a child's needs and doing her best to keep the child safe. This is how the Guardian Angel, feels about you, as this is a good comparison from the one to the other. This is my perspective, of the job of a Guardian Angel, which undertakes as his/her responsibility.

I personally, experienced some near death moments; as outlined previously, but I always felt someone or somebody, was there in my corner. Speaking to Me! This inner feeling, of telling me to fight, to exist! Not to panic, as this was not my time to die! MY NUMBER WASN'T UP?

Just imagine, it as your own personal bodyguard, who is always with you. They would do all the usual bodyguard things, like protecting you from danger; warding off assailants, and generally keeping you safe, in all situations. But, he/she does more than this; they offer you moral guidance; helping you become a stronger person, and leads you, to your ultimate calling in life.

I would now, like to insert some stories of people, who have had an experience, with the Guardian Angel.

Two guys were sitting at a traffic light one night, when the car just stalled. They both got out of the car, to push it into the parking lot of a gas station.

We were having trouble getting the car up the incline. A jogger came out of nowhere; and went on the other side of the car, to where the boys were. He helped push the car up the incline, into the parking lot; and then he just took off. Just then, a car appeared speeding around a curve, and blew right through the intersection. This was exactly, where the car had been moments before. Had this stranger, not helped us move the car, we would have been struck by this vehicle. We both turned around, but the stranger was totally gone; just disappeared into thin air. WE both believe that he was a Guardian Angel, sent to protect us that night!

Another experience, that a young girl remembered, was rolling her car, when she was a teenager. Mid roll, she was taken out of the car and sort of "floated" over the road; until she was placed, feet first on the ground. She later noticed she had bruises, resembling hand prints, on both her biceps. No other bruises or scares on her body from that accident. Her Guardian Angel was on Duty!

There was this man, driving in a winter white out conditions; and typically, you kind of get hypnotized by the snow. He said he heard someone, calling him by his nickname; and he woke up, to discover he was on the wrong side of the road. He was just about to hit an oncoming car. Luckily, he managed to move out of the way, just in time. The man remarked afterwards, that he thought; that the voice he heard; was his grandfather, who had passed away. I always felt, like he is watching over me. My Guardian Angel was on Duty!

There is an incident, which is normal in all respects; of two young girls heading home from school. They were about to cross a country road, which was normally deserted. Having been told, by their parents, to be extremely careful; when crossing the road, but been deserted; they we're not concerned. The one young girl, got to the road, and was overcome with immense sense of dread. She felt like she couldn't move, as if something was literally; holding her at the side of the road.

Her friend, without her, started to cross over the road; and left her there by herself. A guy, in a truck happened to be speeding along; not paying attention, and ran over her friend; and she was killed instantly.

The young surviving girl's mother believes that her Guardian Angel saved her daughter's life, that day! Why, was the other young girl not saved? Could it simply be that HER NUMBER was up, and her time, had come to leave this earth?

A woman couldn't but count her blessings, as she watched a huge tree limb; come crashing down on her car. The very car she was about to get into. Her phone had started to ring, which took her away from the car; and the tree limb just plummeted, leaving the car a mangled mess. Later, it was discovered that the tree looked rotten at the bottom. If it wasn't for the phone call to deal with; I would have been in the car, and dead. I believe I have a Guardian Angel looking after me!

If you ever missed "death" by an inch; and believe you had a little help, you're not alone; like me, you believe in Guardian Angels!

These stories make each and every one of us, to stop for a moment; to consider, the existence of Guardian Angels! To then, think and appreciate GOD and HIS messengers; for all they can do for us. They somehow, just appear in the nick of time? There isn't for this author, any other evidence; or lack of evidence, which disproves the theory; that Guardian Angel doesn't exist!

I am a firm believer, in been given a NUMBER at birth and that a Guardian Angel; is assigned to you. They are there to care for you, in good and bad times, and hopefully to be worthy; when your NUMBER comes up to die. I personally hope, that there is a chance; that I can spend my eternity, with those I loved and miss so terribly.

At this moment, I would like to take a little liberty and stray slightly; from what I was previously writing about. It's a little different slant, to the GUARDIAN ANGEL subject, which I experienced first-hand!

To this end, I am now introducing another book I wrote, entitled "Now You Have Her.....Now You Don't". This takes you on a personal walk, through a widower's grief; as I sadly miss her smile, her love, her very presence in my life.

In undertaking the writing of this book, I have attempted to face the challenges; of losing my partner-in-life. This book is a tribute to my lady; but also a search for some inner peace, comfort and a sense of closeness, to the loved one. She is now departed and has left me with a large void, in my life.

Before, you can begin the pathway through GRIEF; I feel we must first go back to the beginning of the relationship, with your partner. For it's at this point; you will first be able to get in touch, with YOUR inner self; and is in essence, the beginning of your emotional connection.

Like an iceberg, the very tip of which is seen above the surface; so also are your life's emotions—the very heart of that special emotion, called LOVE; is only seen on the surface.

The loss of someone, or something meaningful, precipitates the state of bereavement and mourning. The grieving process results, varies widely in intensity; depending on the nature of what was lost.

There is a widely accepted theory, that "Grieving People"; enter a series of stages, as they grieve.

1. DENIAL
2. ANGER
3. BARGAINIG
4. DEPRESSION
5. ACCEPTANCE

My perception of grief was like travelling down a dark and lonely trail. It was something I had to do on my own, without assistance from outside sources. There was no proper or improper method, map or schedule about the "HOW"; I was to endure it. There is no guide book, about its effects on me or those around me! I had to learn to cope on a daily basis—ONE DAY AT A TIME!

Losing one's soulmate is just like being a ship, which is floundering, caught on a reef. You spend many years, tears and heartaches forming this bond, functioning as one; working for the betterment of both. You're now moving forward in life, as a single entity, on the Sea of Life. You overcome life's speed bumps and its obstacles always looking, for comfort, support and direction.

You reassure each other, that all is well and that in the end; everything will be the way it's supposed to be! When a death of a partner comes, you are never ready! You become like that ship, sinking into a watery grave, which for us is called GRIEF.

I am now a man, or in actual fact, a "shell' of a man; having no interest in life. I didn't want to take any active part in life, not really wanting to be "in life" at all. I think this is what might be called deep depression? I neither cared for the present, nor for my future existence. This is to show case to you the reader, how I went into grief. I didn't know what would be my life, or my existence, in this thing called life?

Four very prominent feelings, which I wish to share and was feeling; not openly expressing, but totally affecting my mental capacity, is the following:

> I AM ALONE
> > I AM SCARED
> > > I AM UNHAPPY
> > > > I AM UNLOVED

Welcome to the "GRIEF ZONE".

Grief is also individualized. How people grieve depends on:

1. The nature of their relationship with the one who died
2. The presence of a support system
3. Previous losses in their lives

4. Religious and spiritual background
5. Cultural beliefs about how to grieve

No one grieves quite like anyone else! No one resolves grief, quite like anyone else either! The ability, to use grief; to reach a new level of experience, is also a variable.

This then brings us to the concept of HOPE. Hope is a vital spiritual need. Hope is willingness to embrace all of life's possibilities. It is suggested that hope is energy; that a lack of hope is a wish to die!

Hope means there is a future! Hope is correlated with a feeling of well-being. A general kind of hope, for the best possible life; under these conditions, is as useful; as hope that has a more defined goal.

AS far as I am concerned, you must move forward. Do not Stagnate! Be the best you can be, as your happiness depends on you; BUT, do it for your very life. Your very happiness depends on this action. Now you have to find, your personal values. Bringing them to the surface and then proceed to build confidence, and pride in yourself. You still can be a "Person of Worth"!

How a surviving spouse copes, depends on the nature of the life, they had together. It also depends on the nature of the death and on the environment. Factors associated with spouses, who do NOT move through grief and continue to have difficulty; for a prolonged period of time, include the following:

1. The sudden and ultimate death of a spouse
2. Multiple losses
3. A high dependency on the deceased
4. A perceived lack of support
5. Poor health prior to bereavement

At this point, I highly recommend a referral to a social worker. I visited one and believe you me; there is no shame, in taking this course of action. I found it extremely beneficial to "bare my soul", express my emotions; open my heart—the very essence of myself!

During this time, immediately following the death of your spouse; the communication skill of "listening"; helps to identify, the importance of such ideas as WHAT WILL I DO NOW?

First and foremost, you have to realize that you are different. You now have made the first step in the healing process; when you put yourself in harmony; with your feelings, thoughts, and actions. You start to discover yourself; but in reality, you are rediscovering yourself!

Now its "YOU" instead of "US" you were so use to! Now the reconnecting to yourself, the real you; can begin to sink in; along with your feelings, your hopes, and your dreams.

This is the beginning point, of your individual quest; into the New Sea of Life's Journey. This is where the waves of life's ups and downs, will now test, every fibre of your being. Not for one moment, am I suggesting that you forget your partner! I know I never well!

Those memories will always be in your "Special Sanctuary of Memories". They will always be tucked away in your heart and mind; always ready to be recalled; to help regain the calm, inner peace needed. This refuse will help, when life's challenges are weighing heavy on you. They remain your personal "comfort and contentment zone"! This is a place for you to visit, before you return to life; and now having been refreshed; you're ready, to face the current daily demands of life.

To this end, I needed to pull myself together; to find the real me again; to begin life anew, and to be part of life. I no longer wanted, to be just a distant shadow, of non-existence. I reached into the depths of my inner soul, touched my heart, and reached for the dormant brain; to restart its engine. I should be working on all eight cylinders, not just the two; currently in use, in my daily life!

I decided to write a poem, to ease my pain, and to express my inner feelings; of my life with grief. The title of my poem, which is shown below, can be read on the following page.

THE PROCESS OF GRIEF

One's grief never ends, but is always a constant in your life.
Although a pathway in your life, it's not a place you wish to stay.
It does not reflect as weakness, nor a lack of faith in God.
It remains the price of love you gave, for your love in return.
As a partner you possessed my body, soul and mind.
But in the end you were kind and left it for me to still possess.
You were my inspiration and my inner peace.
You were my centre point of balance, of reason and of thought.
You left me your courage, my shield from all these wounds.
To help me build my inner strength and have determination.
Your final gift you gave me, to aid me on my way.
As I now forge through life alone.
Your presence always felt, just a mere thought away.
You gave my soul some peace, before you slipped away.
Your spirit still lingers deep within my mind.
A place of total solitude and a resting place for my heart.
You will always be with me; my spirit and heart are yours.
For without you in my mind, I surely would fall apart.
Rest now my love one; be at peace at long last.
Know you're not forgotten, as only your body has left.
You'll always be with me, till our spirits reconnect.

Author: Stephen Paul Tolmie

A NEW BEGINNING! (STARTING YOUR LIFE OVER)

I have related, to the fact that you MUST, now move on in your life! The proverbial words…."Life goes on"…ring true! But, are you going on with your life? Believe me, this is easier said than done.

I have alluded, to the fact that my wife told me to move on in my life; to find satisfaction, or a purpose for my existence. She also said that she wanted me to share my life, with another human being. Her last words still echo in my head "You will always have the memories of us together; my love for you, and her emotions, to help guide me in my life's quest." In reality, it isn't that easy to carry on in life! I knew I could always, reach into my memories of her and take comfort from her and our life together. I knew I would have her for all eternity; in the special place in my heart and mind. The last words to me were "Know that I will always be with you; and be there to console you, give you comfort, peace and security. Her final words to me were that I should find the strength, to move forward in life." MY PERSONAL GUARDIAN ANGEL!

Now, I ask you, to look at YOUR LIFE ….Where is it Now? Take stock in the direction you wish to go? I don't doubt that the walls of uncertainty have started to build around you? They probably make you feel almost claustrophobic?

How do you bring these walls down? How do you find the ability, to take that first step? This is the beginning, into the unknown and untested zone of uncertainty. To a place where your life, will now take on a whole new meaning!

WELL…."Come on down"…and let's build a life—a new Comfort Zone! This is a place, where you will now rediscover yourself. You will be looking for your specific desires and your plans for the future. Your very purpose in this thing called "LIFE!" In this new life, you will have absolutely no control; of its impact on your feelings, your thoughts, and what you perceive; as the "correct" path to follow, in achieving your goals. This new life should be more than just a "BARE EXISTENCE"? You should aspire to achieve contentment, happiness; and live out the rest of your days, with a SENSE of Actually Living Life!

My "GUARDIAN ANGEL" had finally arrived and was making me aware of her presence in my life; telling me to move on and be strong; encouraging me to have faith, and to count on her always, being in my corner.

Something, very important to remember; is that "GRIEF" is never something you get over. You don't just one day wake up, and say is it over; and now I can move on, without PAIN in my heart. It is something that will always be with you; and walks every day in your mind and heart, for your life time. You have to realize, now that everything changes; and life will never be the same again!

I would now, like to close out this portion of my book, with these special last thoughts:

REMEMBER THAT ALTHOUGH HER/HIS BODY HAS BEEN REMOVED FROM YOU; THEIR SPIRIT WILL ALWAYS REMAIN IN YOUR HEART AND MIND, UNTIL YOU ARE ONCE AGAIN REUNITED!!

MEMORIES ARE LIKE KEEPSAKES. THEY ARE ALWAYS TO BE TREASURED!

I would now like to share the eulogy, which I wrote for my wife. To both help heal me; to bond these thoughts to my mind and to express hope, and desire for my future. Now without her presence in my life!

I hope in reading this that you also can relate, to your departed loved one. Possibly, it brings back those special memories to the forefront of your mind? I truly hope, somehow my message will be healing; helpful and honour your memory; which you have of the departed loved one.

HUSBAND'S EULOGY TO HIS WIFE

Now is the hour of pain.
Its presence is eminent in my heart.
The weight of sorrow is heavy.
There seems no relief from its weight.
Time is heavy on our being,
and relief from suffering seems distant.
Hold on! Hold on to good thoughts.
Be consumed by them. Hold tight!
There will be a tomorrow.
And a day after that, and that…
Healing is a slow process.
Take pleasure in the fact that you knew her,
and loved her, as she knew and loved you back.
Remember her laugh, her smile, her wit.
She could lift your spirit and make you feel alive…
or put you in you in line and wish you weren't.
She touched those who came into her world
and left her mark.
Our world will be none the better with her passing,
but she did leave us a piece of her….
But when one looks back on those memories
She is not lost to us.
She will always have our hearts
She will always be in our minds.
She will always be in our prayers.
Life will be able to go on for us.
as she is with us now and forever.

Be at peace my wife……….Your still with us!!

I would now, like to introduce another book; which I wrote, "That Single
Moment"; which explores the four concepts of "GRIEF".

CONNECTING TO GRIEF
COPING WITH GRIEF
CONQUERING GRIEF
CONTINUING LIFE without GRIEF

I wrote this book, to help heal myself, after I lost my wife. I created a fictional character, which I named "Scotty"; portraying myself, through this character. This helped in connecting to my inner feelings and to finally be able to bring them to the surface; in my healing process.

As a short story, I have tried to indicate, how this man works his way through these four elements. I have also attempted to create some poetry; to add some human emotional touch, and to show its impact on his life. This is an effort, to show how it reduces the very meaning of life, to an almost non entity! As he temporarily walks away, from the present world, to an unknown world. This new world of the homeless is one where people are unloved; uncared for and often unrecognized, as human beings. These people only seem to exit, but really don't count in society's standards; of what real life, actually is like!

My fictional character is there to try and cope with life; to help heal himself and search for some actual meaning for his life? Although, this may seem extreme; it obviously, is not everyone's course of action.

We need to respect life, because the very essence of life asks—NO DEMANDS—that you become a person of self-worth; and continue to contribute to life and society. "What if I try and fail?" Ask yourself "What if I never try?" Believe me, it is better to have tried and failed, than to never have tried at all! This is the actual beginning—the start of your new quest, on what is called the "SEA of LIFE"!

In this journey, these waves of lives ups and downs; will again, test every fibre of your being!

It's important in the healing process; to connect to your friends for support, understanding, comfort, and feeling close to another human being.

Through friends and their friendship; you become who you are, what you are; and what you yet may become, because of their guidance and support.

I wrote this poem to my imaginary friend "Scotty", who allowed me to become myself again, and return to life.

FRIENDSHIP

Some people walk in and out of your life, while others leave their mark.
We're always seeking something else, passing the gift of friends so dear
I was blessed to have you as my friend, with whom I grown so close.
To you my friend, I'd like to say, your friendship meant the most.
As I share this thought with you, you'll know it's from my heart.
Your gift to me was priceless—the value of infinity.
How happy, I was to have known you and now life's empty without you.
I pray the Lord to keep you, until we re-connect.
We must learn the mistakes of others, as life
doesn't give a second chance.
The circle of friends should be endless; as in no beginning and no end.
Our yesterdays are now our history; tomorrow is strictly a mystery?
Seize today and simply say.........
Friends are you and me; from now throughout all eternity.

Author: Stephen Paul Tolmie

I would also, for you reading pleasure, like to insert another poem I wrote. I feel that it hits the mark, in describing what friendship truly means to me. It does in fact make the "Point" of having one's back; not leaving a person in the lurch, always to be counted on; always reliable and having the other's person best interest; in your heart as well.

A FRIEND WHO'S ALWAYS THERE

If I could catch a rainbow
I would do it just for you
and share with you its beauty
on the days your feeling blue.

If I could build a mountain
you could call your very own....
a place to find serenity
a place to be alone.

If I could take your troubles
I would toss them in the sea.
But all these things I'm wanting
are impossible for me.

I cannot build a mountain
or catch a rainbow fair;
But let me be what I do best....
Be a friend who's always there!

Author: Stephen Paul Tolmie

WHAT IS LIFE?

You have been given this gift, through a Devine Power
It is a gift to be appreciated and be respectful of
It allows you, to be what you wish, to make of yourself
It makes you realize, that there will be pitfalls and triumphs
You have an opportunity, a desire, and the will power
to complete it
This is not to be taken lightly or misconstrued as a game to play
You will experiences sorrow, pain, and loss and must overcome
You must appreciate this gift and time, to do your best
You will have struggles, tasks to complete, accept this venture
You will experience loss, deaths, and heartache, confront it!
This is your time to shine, the adventure of living life
You have been given a number at birth, be mindful of this fact!
Be all you can be, and enjoy your time spent on earth
There is an ending, to all you have been given!

So in simplicity to this logic, it can be summarized this way:

Live simply, love generously
Care deeply and speak kindly
Be happy within yourself
Take time to smile within yourself, and with others
Life is rich and full, you only get one chance

Author: Stephen Paul Tolmie

I would now, wish to thank you the reader; for allowing me, to reflect on the grief process. Creating a fictional character, allows someone going through this sorrow; a different slant on the healing process! Hopefully, it is beneficial as a source document? To help aid you, when you lose a loved one. To offer some comfort from your pain; and sorrow, which you are currently experiencing.

Possibly, it throws a totally different slant; on the understanding, which you may be going through? I hope that it does help, with the steps in releasing the hold on you; of the pain of GRIEF! This grief seems now to be your whole world! I would now, like to insert a poem which I wrote, which sort of covers the whole meaning; of a loss of a partner, soul mate and the love of your life. Her/his voice will still echo, Her/his memory will still live on as She/ he will always live in your heart; your lives will still be connected; heart to heart and soul to soul!

MISSING YOU

MY life is now hollow
And full of loneliness
I need you in my life
To make my life exist
As you have the ability
To turn my life around
To seek another tomorrow
Knowing when my life is done
A life with you exists

Author: Stephen Paul Tolmie

Now, I would like to close out my thoughts; my looking at grief, with a more positive outlook, to the future. Hopefully, this reflects a point of moving on in your life? I created a poem, which I feel reflects the new beginning; or at least a new perspective, on you moving forth in life.

MY PERSONAL GOAL

I long to stride in sunshine
to show kindness to all I should meet.
Though I may be carrying a burden
that many are unable to see.

For if life has given me a reason
to cry and carry pain;
then I will look for that pathway
to be able to smile and find myself again.

To find a new horizon;
to seek new goals in life;
to strive to be a better person;
too long to be whole once again.

And find that lost rainbow;
to seek out life's lost treasures
with a new soul-mate in my life,
to hold, to love, to share, to care…..
to finally be at peace myself
and regain my life again.

Author: Stephen Paul Tolmie

I would now, like to add my personal thoughts; which I try to follow in my everyday life. This is sort of my handbook, guide and directions in moving forward in life. I hope you may be able to apply, some of these thoughts, or suggestions in your life; and the rebuilding of your life. They may not be applicable, but at the least, they may make you, Stop and Think? To say these words, "Yes, I see the merit to this logic or common sense, and it does have some significance/meaning; as applied to my life"?

I hope there are enough sunny days, to keep your attitude bright

I hope there's enough happiness, to keep your spirit on high

May there be enough friction in your life, to appreciate life more

May you receive enough in life, to satisfy you're wanting?

May the loss you experience, make you more aware of what you have?

May there be enough greetings in your life, which fill that need

May your strength be there, to get you through, the final goodbyes?

Author: Stephen Paul Tolmie

These final thoughts, which I wish to passing along, are for your consideration, validation and for food for thought. I feel this material kind of sums it up, this moving forward portion into your new life; as how you look at life; feel life, and even go through life.

Life has a way of taking away all the non-essential possessions, we think we need in our lives; until we are left, with what is the basics, "our real selves". This is how the world and other people perceive us. We all hope that we have learned, with all life's experiences, and have shaped into, what we are today? We now know what we know, we love what we love, and we continue striving, to reach that Golden Ring of Success. This represents our true reality of happiness; been successful and having a contented life style, which completes our lives.

The bottom line is we all think we have great quantities; of this precious commodity, called TIME. We hope it's enough, enough indeed; to be all we could/should be; and in truth, the fact is, it should be!

Always remember, you have been given a NUMBER at birth; so don't lose this thought, and live every day as it could be! Please don't squander your time away, make it count; leave your foot print that you were in fact here; and did in truth leave… YOU'RE PERSONAL MARK!!

I would be amidst, if I didn't include another of my books; entitled "Estate Planning & Executor Guide". This book deals with the many procedures, explanations and documents required; when handling one's affairs; before and after their passing.

This is merely a suggestion, for helping in the healing and closure process. I found expressing my feelings was easier, than speaking to a family member; a friend or a consultant.

I wrote this poem, in an effort to show; how one slowly connects, to a special person in one's life. Then, they experience that loss; leaving a huge void; and uncertainty, now, where indeed; do you go from here?

WILL YOU REMEMBER ME

You came into my world, when there was pain and sorrow.
You intensely listened. You seemed to care.
You stated your opinion, to always be there.
We shared good times and bad.
We drifted emotionally apart,
Then like a tide, returning, we slowly touched again.

Our emotions still intact, we seemed very cautious.
We seemed unprepared, to touch one another's life,
But, we felt a bond emerging.
A new desire, which began to grow

Will our lives connect, or strictly just be friends?
Will another tide take you from me?
Will my world end?
Will pain and sorrow once again appear?
To then, fill my life's existence?
Will emotions never end?

Author: Stephen Paul Tolmie

Now, we begin the process of learning about "Estate Planning & Executor Guide".

I suggest we take it step by step, to realize the total picture. The whole realm of what is involved? Looking at either your life's wishes, at your demise; your loved ones, friends or whatever the case may be?

Your executor needs information, on where to find you're WILL; which should be his/her first priority! This is the main document, to first address their full attention to! Also knowing the existence of any other special documents, which need immediate attention? Your estate inventories, specifically their location, are mandatory for quick processing!

You can't imagine how much time can be lost, just in looking for financial information. Also, the immediate worry about funeral arrangements, with no idea of the source of these documents. Putting your affairs in order; gives your executor, a road map to move ahead more efficiently. With your estate planning, it makes you think about what you have; and who you want it to go to, after you pass. It is important, to document this information with your lawyer! Making sure, there are no issues that need addressing; or second guessing by the executor. This will help; give you a little better understanding, of some of the issues that will arise. The saying "For Warned is For Armed" and having a little knowledge, is always very beneficial!

DO YOU NEED ESTATE PLANNING?

What is Estate Planning?
What is involved in Estate Planning?
Who needs Estate Planning?
What is included in my assets?
What is a WILL?

What is a "Revocable Living Trust?
What is Probate?
To whom should I leave my assets?
Whom should I name as my Executor or Trustee?
How should I provide for my children?
When does Estate Planning involve Tax Planning?
How does the way in which I hold title, make a difference?
What are other methods of leaving property?
What if I become unable to care for myself?
Who should help me with my Estate Planning documents?
How do I find a qualified lawyer?
Should I become aware, of someone who is a promoter, such as Financial and Estate Planning services?
What are the costs involved in Estate Planning?

This is just a SAMPLE, of some of the questions you should be asking yourself; as it is never too early, to put down your ideas? This also, is a good indicator of your thinking process. Organizing your assets, for your loved one; should be something that you are totally prepared for.

WILLS AND POWER OF ATTORNEY!

A WILL, is a written document, giving instructions for the disposition of your property; after death and appoints a personal representative; called an "EXECUTOR"; to deal with the property on your behalf. A properly drawn up- to- date WILL; is one of the finest protections you can give to your family!

Your lawyer will be able to assist you in drafting a WILL, to reflect your wishes.

It is advisable that everyone should have a WILL; in order to have control, over the distribution of his/her property. In absence of a WILL, application must be made; to the court, to appoint an ADMINISTRATOR! He/she would then fulfill the duties; which would normally have been done, by an appointed executor.

DUTIES OF AN EXECUTOR!

Just what does it mean to be an executor? A simple explanation is that he/she has been named in a WILL; to handle an estate, when someone dies. The size and many aspects of an estate, especially; as to how well the person's affairs are in order; can prove to be easy, or can become a difficult, and a time consuming process, for the executor!

Any person, who has been asked to take on this task; should be well aware, as to what it means, and all that is involved?

POSSIBLE DUTIES OF
AN EXECUTOR!

Find, read and interpret the WILL
Consult with the lawyer and arrange probate (court validation)
of the WILL.
Help with funeral arrangements if necessary
Locate and deal with beneficiaries named in the WILL
Prepare an inventory of the deceased's assets and liabilities
Deal with financial institutions and contracts-including
banks insurance companies and pension plans.
Distribute assets as specified in the WILL. This may involve
selling real estate; or other property, if cash bequests are specified.
Pay debts and estate expenses.
Place advertisements to find creditors
Apply for Canada Pension Plan benefits
File the deceased's final income tax returns

This is some and maybe not all the duties; which an executor may have to undertake. As in all cases, not everyone is the same; be it simple to process or difficult. It also, may involve getting professional help; to provide the necessary advice, to carry out those specific instructions.

WHO SHOULD YOU CONSIDER SELECTING AS YOUR EXECUTOR?
A trusted family member
A friend
A non-family member
Your personal lawyer
A Trust Company
Your Financial Advisor

These are merely SOME SUGGESTIONS to consider? The main thing in chosen your executor is to know you can trust him/her 100%; whoever you choose? These are your final wishes, which you want carried out; and once you're gone; there is no rewrite, or changing your mind! One thing I would like to STRESS, is that whoever; your executor is; has the predominant skills, in Both Written and Oral Communication!

Two other documents, which should be noted; apart from the WILL; are The Power of Attorney and Power of Attorney for Personal Care!

POWER OF ATTORNEY, allows that person appointed; to ACT on your behalf; to do all your personal and business responsibilities; (LEGAL RIGHT to sign YOUR NAME). This document shouldn't be taken lightly, but with deep thought on your part!

POWER OF ATTORNEY FOR PERSONAL CARE, allows that person to act on your behalf; when you are NOT physically or mentally capable; of looking after yourself; (basically a MEDICAL DIRECTIVE). Again, this document shouldn't be taken lightly, but with an immense amount of consideration!

I am merely noting these two documents, as although "VERY IMPORTANT", some readers; may not be aware of their existence? You should definitely seek the help of your lawyer, to have them in place.

You should also prepare a list, as a guide to what items; your executor may require, in executing you're WILL! Once your list is completed, and your family told that it exists; and where it is kept; it should be updated at least once a year!

Examples of important documents, needed by your executor; to just mention as few are:

Your Marriage certificate
Your Birth certificate
Your Death certificate
You're Social Insurance Number
Safety Box location
Name of bank, box number and where keys are kept
Burial plans, Cemetery Deeds
Last WILL and Testament Documents
Most recent income tax returns
Auto registration or lease agreements
Any property deeds, partnerships or trust agreements
Any divorce or separation agreements
Any pre-nuptial or post nuptials agreements
List of credit cards, in separate or joint names
Recent statements of mutual funds, securities
stocks in separate or in joint names
A list of insurance policies (health, home, car & life)
A list, of the most recent statements, for any
chequing or saving accounts; in either separate or
joint name.
A list, of debts, along with the most recent mortgage
statements (if applicable).

In providing this list, of potential documents; that may be needed, it is just that; and only a GUIDE! There may be something I have left out, or many items mentioned; aren't applicable? In each case; it has to be weigh upon its own merits? This is, to show case ONLY; what may be needed, as an INFORMATION TOOL!

MY FINAL THOUGHT!

I hope, I have giving you motivation; in deciding your wishes; for your Estate Distribution, Your WILL, Power of Attorney and Power of Attorney for Personal Care! My intentions were Two Fold? To make you THINK, and then to ACT UPON YOUR WISHES; so that nothing is left to chance? This is so important, not only to you; but to assist your loved ones; knowing what needs to be done, and how you wish them to go about it! It helps to show; that your last thoughts were your love for them and your wishes to see them looked after; when you are gone. This also, eases the pain of decision making on their part; as the workbook format, can be easily followed. The information provided, will help your family deal, with your loss, and in essence; still put them in touch with you.

I hope I have shed some light, and insight into your Personal Estate Planning? My attempt was to show the myriad of things, which may become necessary to complete; when a loved one dies. This can be a STRESSFUL TIME!

If in some small way, I have helped to lift the burden and stress at this most difficult time; then my time has been well spent; on this subject!

REMEMBER THAT ALTHOUGH HER/HIS BODY HAS BEEN REMOVED FROM YOU; THEIR SPIRIT WILL ALWAYS REMAIN IN YOUR HEART AND MIND, UNTIL YOU ARE REUNITED ONCE AGAIN!!

In considering, some of the items, that I have briefly outlined in my book; hopefully, they have given you some insight; of your new emotional roller coaster ride? This is strictly an attempt, to inform you; what you will be dealing with; when you deal with death.

This, I feel, all ties into the purpose of this book; "WHEN IS YOUR TIME UP? We have been talking about the subject of death and avoiding the Angel of Death; so allowing me to stray a little from the main stream topic; I felt should be allowed? The other reason, was to give you a heads up; of what is coming, and possibly a new source book available for you to read? This will allow you; to gain insight, healing and preparation, for the inevitable ending, that comes to us all!

Now, let's return to the subject at hand, of "What is a Near Death Experience"?

According to the dictionary, a near death experience is "an unusual experience taking place on the brink of death and recounted by a person on recovery, typically an out of body experience or a vision of a tunnel of light".

Eventually, a person claims to have come close to experiencing death; only to recover, and remember what it is they saw; heard or felt during that experience. Many of the reported near death experiences share similarities, as well as key differences; so there is not a "right" way to have one.

There is no mystery greater, than what lies beyond death! We have no way of knowing what happens when life ends; and those who fully pass beyond its doors, do not return.

But, there are those who have, through great tragedy and pain; had a glimpse of what lies beyond. These people, who have been as close to clinical death as possible; and have been revived. When they return, they brought back words of what they saw.

There's incredible comfort in this—the reassurance that life doesn't end after death; that there might be something more, is heartwarming. It's wonderful to be reminded, that our departed loved ones; are waiting for us, and that behind it all; there a sense of peace and tranquillity. For those who are on the fence, concerning faith, personal narratives or near death experiences; this can hopefully, help push in the right direction. These experiences tend to be remarkably consistent in their details---too consistent, for even the staunchest materialist to ignore.

We all, at times need that kind of boost to our faith! Most of us walk through life, without ever seeing a hint; of the supernatural. To hear stories, of encounters with the afterlife in general; can be just the faith pick me up we need!

I would now, like to reflect on some stories; I have heard of people having a near death experience, and describing that experience.

A man, who was critically ill, and he said he felt himself; lift from his body and was staring down at his body; in the bed. He said he experienced falling through space, and into a bright white light. I was aware of a radiant being; in a long white robe, and thought immediately of Jesus; from the pictures, I had seen of him in church. When I returned to my body, I felt more mentally and physically drained; than I had ever in my lifetime. Now, I realized that I had just experienced the first stage of dying!

There was a man, who had a severe epileptic seizure, and as a result; was on a life support system in the hospital. He stated he found himself standing at the foot of my bed, and looking at myself. I thought to myself, been this is the end; just go with the flow, and you will wake up in a wonderful world of peace and happiness. Then, out of nowhere, a voice started telling me; that I had obligations to fulfill, and I realized I was going back into my body. I heard, one of the doctor's exclaim "Thank God"; he's beginning to show signs of life at last!

Since that experience, I have rethought my attitude towards death.

Another incident, where a man had a massive heart attack; and during this period of pain, I saw a white figure; hovering over me. This image seemed to be in a white robe, and I couldn't distinguish the face. As this image drew closer, I saw the face of my brother; who had been killed in the war. This appearance, although brief; was clear and vivid to me. When I recovered there was nothing. As this was a personal experience, between when I was close to death; and my brother coming to greet me, it reinforced my belief; that there is something positive after death.

A woman suffered a fracture skull and fell into a deep coma. She experienced a long dark tunnel, and a cloaked figure coming her way. Follow me; were the words, and as we walked; we soon came out of the tunnel, into a brilliant light. I was viewing a lovely garden, trees, pool of water, a stream running by, and birds singing. I was so totally at peace, and didn't want to leave.

Then a voice said, "You have to go back now". I felt, when I returned back to my body; that this experience truly happened to me, and that it wasn't a dream. I felt, I did go through the valley of death, and reached the gates of heaven. I realized, that I had a near death experience; and now feel comforted, when my time is up.

Then, there are yet another story; where a sister had died, and the remaining sister; had been taken seriously ill. She was in the hospital and nearly died on the operating table. They removed me from the intensive care unit, and placed me back into a ward room; where I had a frightening experience. An old man, was standing at the side of my bed; and I was having a full conversation with him. He was stating it wasn't my time to go! A woman, in the next bed, heard the whole conversation; that I was saying, and the woman was quite hysterical. There wasn't anybody there! Yet, another near death experience; not as descriptive as the others, previously mentioned. Still, who was this mystery figure; an Angel, a relative, or another distant family member? Was this figure sent to tell this lady, Her Time Was Not Up?

There is a brief account, of a man dying; and feeling his spirit body rise up over his physical body; and feeling full of joy, and brimming with health. My "real" body below, looked in a very sorry state; and I didn't want to return. Eventually, I did, and survived. There is no mention from him of any tunnels, bright lights or meeting relatives; just this out of body; near death experience.

There is a story of a man in the hospital, and in so much pain; that he actually was asking God, to let him die. When I was at my lowest point, I found that I was looking down at myself; from the corner of the room.

I was near the ceiling, and seen a doctor come into my room and give me an injection. I had no connection to any other mental thoughts. Just that God had answered my prayers to die. The most shocking thing was that I wasn't, the slightest bit scared of dying. In all honesty, I felt totally at peace within myself. I felt that a heavenly power was there to take away the existing pain. Once the injection kicked in, I was then returned to my body; to face further treatment.

To the next story of a woman, after having a serious operation; had the feeling, of leaving her body and floating upwards; just like a feather.

It was a wonderful, warm and comforting experience. She stated she heard music a long way off; and ahead of me, was a marble staircase with men, woman and children descending. The music I heard was them singing. I was about to put my foot on the bottom step, when I heard my husband's voice calling me. I saw him, standing in the hospital hallway; talking with a nurse. I was heartbroken to come back, but now; I have no fear of death. This also, is another near death experience; but having some common elements; of floating in the air, with music, singing, and the introduction of a marble staircase. This is just another little twist, in some of the other mentioned to this point.

There was a story of a man, having a usual habit of going for a night walk; as a way to unwind from his day at work. Unfortunately, one night, he slipped and fell down a steep hill. Although, severely injured with 23 broken bones and a broken skull; he was still able to get himself back up, from the ravine.

He was lying by the side of the road dying, when suddenly; a bright blinding light appeared to him. Although, the bright light was shining on him; it still had a comforting and softness to it. It was as though; the light was somehow, holding me in its arms. From this bright light, stepped a figure-God; and the pain started to subside and my breathing became easier. The man had thought that God, had come to take him to heaven; and he was saddened to leave his family. God reassured him though; that "it wasn't his time yet to leave"!

The man made it to safety that night, and after many surgeries, recovered. He now uses his near death experience; to give others hope and light, he himself received; during his brush with death.

Finally, to a story of a woman, who went kayaking? She had gone completely over a small waterfall. When reaching the bottom of the waterfall, was pushed down; by the tremendous ferocity, that it had.

She was stuck, eight feet under the existing water surface. In a brief moment, she was overtaken by a sense of comfort and reassurance; saying "I believe Christ was holding me"!

She went on to describe, been greeted by a group of benign spirits who were overjoyed to see her; welcomed and protected her. She stated, that she felt she was on the threshold of death, and felt a powerful love been generated; from the other side. In reality, it simply wasn't her time; and the spirits told her so! She awoke, with someone giving her mouth to mouth resuscitation, and to a number of broken bones and torn ligaments. The entire way to the hospital, she stated; she felt no pain. The lady now states, that she will never forget the intense feeling of being unconditionally loved; that radiated from those in Heaven.

An Amazing Near Death Experience!

How impactful, these near death experiences! Hopefully, they have given some comfort; a stronger belief in the after world, and that there is an eternity. Death does not end it all! Yes, your body is dead, but your spirit; lifts upwards towards heaven. There, hopefully to be reconnected, to all that you long for; in the next phase of your Spirit World.

This should help make you feel better about death, and watching your loved ones pass on. It shouldn't be a painful void, but instead; knowing their Spirit Life will live on. This should be a moment, to reflect; that the person is now out of pain. Accepting the fact, it's just another step in mankind's journey; to a better place of peace, contentment and a reunion; with those that previously passed.

I saw a sign in a store front window, which I would like to pass on:

Life should NOT be a journey to the grave, with the intentions of arriving safely; in an attractive and well preserved body; BUT rather to skid in sideways; body thoroughly used up, totally worn out, and screaming "WOO HOO, WHAT A RIDE"!

In recapping this concept, you shouldn't fear death! You're merely passing through a doorway, from an earthly world; to a heavenly world. Non-believers would probably say; that I am living in a bubble, of another heavenly world. What I would say to them is this: "My Belief is NOT in a total stop; merely blackness, loneliness and isolation; and I prefer to believe, that there is something after death"!

"WHAT'S YOUR THOUGHTS"?

Just a closing thought, as the author; I wonder if it is true, that a record is kept; of your good deeds virus your bad deeds? This indicates, whether you go to Heaven or to Hell. It is said in the Bible, that you go before St. Peter; and he examines your file, to decide your eternity fate. Just thinking out loud, wouldn't it be nice to see your account; and see indeed, where you stand; and have time to correct all your misdeeds? This is not living, and we have to live by our mistakes; and hopefully in the end; when the tally is done, the GOOD outweighs the BAD!

Now, leaving this section on Near Death Experiences; and turning to another book; that I wrote, hopefully for you to explore? In this book, it is a personal exploration of myself, and is entitled: "THE QUEST".

This is where I looked at myself, from the 5 W's (where, when, who, what and why) of my actions taken? The repercussions from my actions taken or not; and whether these actions were good or bad on my part? This is an opportunity, to explore you; through the GOOD and BAD accounts; of your personal life. Your time to prepare yourself, for the after world; and all ties in, with the title of the book "WHEN IS YOUR TIME UP?

JUST A SHORT INTERMISSION, BEFORE WE RESUME WITH THE TOPIC AT HAND! I wanted to have a break, and look for a moment; at the brighter side to life! They say "take time to smell the roses" and we are!

I have seen, read, or heard these lines in my lifetime; and wanted to pass them forward, for your consideration. They are very prevalent, to the whole concept of life; wrapped up in these three sentences.

"Life has a way of stripping away all the nonessentials, Until we are left with our real-selves!-Unashamed before the world!

Refined by experience, shaped by the things we've learned"?

YET NOW, ANOTHER SEGMENT; to explore you through, as an examination; of your life time on earth. This is what I like to call, the four season of your life. You have no promise, that in fact; that you will see all the seasons of your life.

The SPRING SEASON of ONE'S LIFE!

Life begins; you walk, talk and observe all that life throws your way.
You experience life and all its challenges.
You learn from your mistakes,
and find reward in your accomplishments.
The learning curve of life,
is set in motion and time moves on.
The roller coaster ride of life,
does, in fact, have it UPS and DOWNS.
The SUMMER SEASON of ONE'S LIFE!

You are now in your 20's 30's and 40's. You have met and lost relationships with girlfriends, male friends; employers and even family members; which have moved away. The family ties grow thinner, as well; as the family member passing away. You're not fixated on anything in particular, as you're young; and have ever changing feelings; for almost everything and everyone.

The FALL SEASON of ONE'S LIFE!

You are now in your 40's 50's and 60's. You are still searching, for that perfect job; the perfect job location and even to a commitment, to a special lady; due to the Summer Season attitude. You're not as committed to a special person. You always think there might be somebody else you may prefer; and have more in common with? You have loved, lost, and shattered their hearts and yours. You have experienced pleasure, sorrow, love and pain. You, secretly long for the restless feeling to subside; and grow more mature, knowing that life is passing you by. It's now, TIME, to grow up; and digest what is happening in life?

The WINTER SEASON of ONE'S LIFE!

You are now in your 60's 70's and 80's. You have at this stage, a strong hope of a partner in your life. You long for that special soulmate and best friend. You long for that special lady to be there, to care, to share, all the remaining happy moments; and life's memories, which you have built together. This has all taken place, through the love for one another; shared happiness and your bond to one another; strictly through time spent together. There is an OLD DUTCH saying; which really comes to mind, and should be shared; for all to appreciate, its absolute meaning!

"TOO SOON OLD, TOO LATE SMART"!

You have NO PROMISE that you will see all the seasons of your life.... SO LIVE FOR TODAY; and say all the things, that you want your LOVED ONES to remember! You hope, that they appreciate and love you; for all the things that you have done for them; in all the years that have passed?

LIFE IS A GIFT TO YOU! The way you live your life, is your gift to those who come after you; so make it a Memorable One! Leave your foot print in the sand, that you were here; and left this world a better place! Knowing you were blessed, to have made that special connection to someone; and have it leave a Lasting Memory!

How you live your life, is very much dependent; on what you identify within yourself; and how others reflect upon you, and your actions. You must learn, from your mistakes, and correct those mistakes. Life doesn't give a Second Chance; to make a Final Lasting Memorial Impression; to leave behind, after your death.

Remember, it is not all about the material items you collected; or your personal wealth, which you will be remembered for? Sure it will be appreciated, but the real wealth; you leave behind, is a TREASURED GOOD MEMORY! This is something, which can be retold over and over; to bring you back, to that family member. This is the TRUE ESSENCE OF; WHAT KIND OF LIFE YOU LIVED!

Yes, I have regrets? There are things I wish I had done, things I should have done; but indeed, there are also many things; which I am happy to have done. IT'S ALL IN A LIFE TIME!

So, if you're not in the winter season yet; let me remind you, that it will be here faster than you think! Whatever, you would like to accomplish in your life; make sure you get it done! Life goes by so quickly, do what you can today. You never can be sure, whether you're closing in on the winter season; or that your NUMBER is soon to be called?

And so.....now I enter, the winter season of my life; unprepared for all the aches, pains and loss of strength. The ability, to go on to do the things that I wish I had done; but never did! I know, that though the winter season has come, and I'm not sure how long it will last; this I know, that when it's over on this earth; it's over? OR IS IT? As I have been stressing in this book, I believe; this is just the beginning, of our journey. Yes, our bodies are dead, but our spirit will go on to the next journey. The start of rekindling, rejoining and nourishing our spirit, with the spirits of our passed loved ones; and to join them for all eternity.

NOW, LET US RETURN TO THE SUBJECT AT HAND! What happens, after death? Many people wonder, marvel and even anticipate; what kind of reality, they will face; when they leave this world! In fact, the emphasis on this is the main stay; for the foundation, for all the world's religions. It seems too incredible, and unreal; to think that this life, with all your intelligence and capabilities; would cease, when your body ceases to function. Somehow, this seems to be a contradiction! It is not merely, that it is fear or anxiety? Yes, correctly it is a contradiction. You were born with a spark of awareness, and you will leave this world; with a spark of awareness.

This mystery surrounding this issue continues to perplex people everywhere; and is of great concern; with every person in this universe. I don't feel there are any misconceptions to living, dying and the after world; which we all don't ponder, to some point or another?

The contemplation, of what might happen; after you leave this world, is certainly on the minds of people; who are facing grave illness. It's certainly, on the minds of many people; who are reaching, the final stages of their life; in this world. It becomes a great emphasis, for everyone; how you lived your life here; before death. It reflects in a large part, in the determination to how you view your overall existence.

There comes a time in your life, when you need to walk away; from all the people; who are causing you stress, anxiety and drama? Then, to turn to those people, who make you laugh; and wanting to partake in life, and all its wondrous moments.

You need to forget; all the times you were unhappy, sad and miserable and change your outlook. Now, turning to the people; who love and treat you right, and respect who you are; and what makes you tick. There is an old saying, which I had read, heard or someone told me; in some portion of my life. Its meaning, stuck with me all these many years.

"Life is too short to be anything but happy, falling down is a part of that life; and getting back up, is living life!"

A moral, I have lived with, and wish to share; as it doesn't matter; how much you obtained in possession and wealth; which tells of your real life. Rather, how much you shared with others, your good fortune; which really tells the true essence; of the kind of life you lived.

My food for thought, which I wish to pass on; for your consideration; is expressed below:

I truly believe, our thoughts control what happens in our life. You have to make your own happiness; control your destiny, and fixate on worthwhile, beneficial and pure deeds. You will then end up; with your own happiness and having a good life. Now, at this point; you can look back on your life; and reflect on what you did, in fact accomplish? Then hopefully, be proud of your course of action; which you took in life.

When you wake up with a happy outlook and a smile on your face; then things will begin to happen in your life. You will then realize you have been given a wonderful gift!

A person should learn from his/her past, use the present; as a tool or engine, where you start moving forward; finally in the right direction. Your future should be your motivation, to accomplish all that you set out to do; in your life time. As the saying goes" You come from dust, and you will return to dust". All you truly have is the existing PRESENT to savor; as your PAST is behind you, and strictly you're FUTURE; is where everybody is heading. Be it GOOD or EVIL, is that person's prerogative!It seems, that most of the time; it is infinitely easier to give advice than to receive it. So to turn to someone and simply say, look for the good in his/her life; is not really providing that person, with a solution. The idea is too broad and in reality, it is just one part of the solution; although a critical aspect, of the solution. In reality, its only one part; as there are many other points to consider. Striving, to the total picture of the problem at hand; is the whole purpose?

Time and security both play a part, in one's ability; to reflect on both good and bad events. A person taking the time, to wipe his/her mind clears of the mundane thoughts and worries; can be the only way, to achieve true reflection. A person shouldn't let the issues or annoyances of the present, distort how you see and evaluate; an event from your past. Once you have cleared your mental place, then you need to know; that no matter what you discover; you have friends and family. They will always be by your side with comfort and support. Reliving bad memories can be as painful; as the day you actually experienced them. All those people who love, support, and encourage you; will give you the strength to seek the good, and to find the lesson in your darkest hour? The key to a Happy Life is choosing to LOOK; for the GOOD!

To realize each experience is a learning tool and not a barrier or excuse for misery. There is no single moment of clarity, when your brain; begins to process in this manner. It entails, your entire life lesson learned; just like taking that first step as a child. This practice, of that specific routine; is what solves your problem of mobility. You don't learn a new skill in a negative environment? This is where people criticize, yell and hurt your feelings; for the mistakes you are making. You need to attain a sense of balance, the security in your life; and knowing your own self-worth. Once you have found that good, secure and happy place, only then; can you take an honest look at yourself? This then, will be a total unbiased look at yourself; to see your actions, and then to learn from your past.

All this material stems from people nearing death; as to whether they will go to heaven, to hell or maybe stay in limbo in purgatory. People start to let their minds wander, as to their own personal lives; did they live a good life? Was it a bad life that they are now ashamed to remember? It is too late to undo all the actions, which they took; and at the moment laughed about? Is it too late for any kind of apologies; or attempt to change their past? Will they get to the PEARLY GATES, and then only to be told; they don't qualify to enter heaven? Will they again see their loved ones? Will this eternal life, be as glorious as they had hoped; and had heard about? Will my death even count, by the people I left behind; after my death? Did I leave with good energy or bad energy, through the life I lived; that my memories will continue on?

These are some thoughts, which I set before you; in deliberation, of what I have been writing about; "WHEN IS YOUR TIME UP? ", and what happens next; in this final process?

Now let us, turn to the PRIME SUBJECT AT HAND; "What happens when we die"? The ground theory has been laid, due to us having explored a lot of subject matter; getting to this point. We have looked at, escaping the Angel of Death; when we had life threatening accidents, and how we're still here. Having also, the experience of the Guardian Angel with us and allowing us to escape death; as our NUMBER wasn't up yet? Again, this is my personal opinion; of being given a number at birth. Then, just like a lottery; we wait sometimes not too patiently; for that number to come up. Sometimes, this idea never crosses our minds; until a situation confronts us. Some people like to think, it was just LADY LUCK; that was on their side? BUT WAS IT?

Sooner or later, that NUMBER has to come up; and now for the rest of the story, as the suspense is killing me; literally!

Should we fear death? Will we be harshly judged and condemned for our sin? Will we experience eternal peace and joy? What is to be our fate?

The question everyone asks themselves; is there really an afterlife? Your body will indeed die, but you are more than your body. You are a spirit, and you are life from God; created to live forever. I now turn to the Bible, for this quote: Jesus said "In my Father's house are many mansions; if it were not so I would have told you. I go now to prepare a place for you." (John 14:2) We are all created, for a unique place in heaven. "Assuredly, I say to you; today you will be with me in paradise."
(Luke 23:43).

When someone we love dies; even those who live a full life in this world; and pass away in old age, we grieve their loss. We cherish our memories, and honour what impact for the good; they had in the world. For those, who find it hard to believe in the afterlife; it can be a very sad time. This presumes that the departed, have really left this world; and never to hear their words; or see their bodies ever again. This doesn't have to be the case. We were created by an external God, we actually can sense; deep within ourselves; that we will never die. Many people instinctively know that there is life after death. Not because they desire it to be so; but because deep within; at the core of their being, they sense it. This perception is built right into us. Can you get in touch with it? I know that I have little doubt in the reality of the afterlife. I feel it, and always have; had this feeling; all my life. I personally have had a glimpse of it; or have been miraculously touched by it; that I can't doubt it. My own personal example, when my grandfather whom I admired; enjoyed his company and thought the world of; passed away. In that very night, I awoke to a feeling of somebody in my room. When I opened my eyes, I seen a silhouette of a man's figure; floating in my room. This figure came close to my bed.

I felt a total calm, peace within myself; and knew I had a connection to this figure. This figure stood very close to me, what seemed like an hour; but in reality, a brief interlude. I received comfort, as my tears that I had been crying; seemed to be dried from my face. I truly felt a strong connection to my grandfather, at that very moment. From this very experience; I have never questioned myself; as to where I will end up; and don't question, that the AFTER WORLD IS REAL!

I now would, like to insert my personal thoughts:

The people we love, don't just go away,
as they walk beside us, in our everyday
They are unseen, and unable to be touched,
we never can speak to them or hear their thoughts.
They are always near to us, in our hearts and our mind,
always very dear to us, still missed and loved.
They remain in our everyday life,
we still have their presence with us.
Our hearts are still saddened,
the tears come from time to time.
We know the pain we felt, when losing you
but know your presence, is still very much with us.

The afterlife (also referred to as life after death) is a belief. The essential part of an individual's identity; or the stream of consciousness; continues after death, of the physical body. There are various ideas about the afterlife, and the essential aspect of an individual; which lives on after death. There may be some partial element, or the entire soul or spirit; of an individual. Belief in the afterlife is in contrast, to the belief; in total oblivion after death.

There are some views, the continued existence; often takes place in a spiritual realm. Others like to think, that the individual may be reborn into this world; and begin the life cycle, all over again. This is with the belief, that they have no memory; of what they had done in the past? In this latter view, such rebirths and deaths may take place over and over continually; until the individual gains entry; in a spiritual realm or "Otherworld." There is also a strong belief, that the dead go to a specific place of existence; after death; as determined by God. Or possibly, another

Devine judgement; based on their actions and beliefs of their life time; states where they go, after death.

Heaven is also, described as a "higher place"; the holiest place; a paradise; in contrast to Hell, or the underworld; or the "low place". Universally or conditionally this can be accessible by earthly beings. This is based on the accordance; to various standards of divinity, goodness, piety, faith or other virtues; or the right beliefs; or simply the will of God. Hell, in many religions; and folkloric traditions; is a place of torment, and punishment in the afterlife. Religions, with a linear divine history; often depict hell, as an external destination. While in other religions, with a cyclic history; often depicts a hell, as an intermediary; between incarnations. Typically, these traditions locate hell in another dimension. This includes entrances to hell from the land of the living.

Other, afterlife destinations; include purgatory and limbo. A lot of people have seen, heard, or felt the presence of death; and then returned back to their bodies. There have been countless studies of individuals, all over the world; who have had near death experiences. Those, who experience this event; have had some sort of contact with the afterlife; when been close to death themselves. Skeptics may call this experience wishful thinking. People of all faiths, even no faith, reported the same conditions; existing over and over again; young and old, of every culture and back ground. They wake up happy, healthy, and whole. They see relatives and friends, and experience a beautiful light. Those, which have been clinically dead for a long time; see cities and lights, beautiful countryside's; and even the presence of angels. It's very interesting, that most of what is recorded; and by those who have had a near death experiences; all conclude, the same story line. There may be slight variations, due to personal beliefs; and the events causing their death; but similarities, still are in existence.

This too, is reflected again and again; in the Bible, as Jesus, assures us that we live on.

"But concerning the resurrection of the dead---have you not read what was spoken to you by God. I am the God of Abraham, the God of Isaac, and the God of Jacob? God is not the God of the dead but the living."
Matthew 22:31-32

Again, in the Bible (a small segment of Psalms 23) there is a saying, which I know by heart:

Yea though I walk through the valley of the Shadow of Death
I will fear no evil
My rod and my staff, they comfort me
Surely goodness and mercy will follow me
All the days of my life
And I shall dwell in the house of the Lord forever.

I would like to insert four poems, on death; which I wrote; to show my emotions of my loss of my wife, soul-mate and best friend. This is to showcase my inner feeling, and display my broken heart. I am now, a hollow man; with her passing and totally feel; a void of existence.

It's very important, to remember; it's ONLY a loss of them, in their present body form. You MUST; remember that their spirit lives on, in your personal heart and mind. All that it takes; to recount them back into your life, is too merely to think of them. Then, your life is renewed; with THEIR presence once again.

I truly hope, in reading these poems; that it rekindles thoughts of your past loved ones? Reliving those extra special moments, to once again; flash back, to your special time; you had with them. I hope it furnishes those cherished memories; and that your heart will be warmed by this experience!

MEMORIES ARE LIKE KEEPSAKES. ALWAYS TO BE TREASURED!

LIVE FOR THE MOMENTS; YOU CAN'T PUT INTO WORDS!

The four poems I wrote; are entitled:

The Empty Hole of Existence

Thinking of You

My Spirit is on High

My Last Thoughts as I leave this Earth

The Empty Hole of Existence

May she always be with you in memory?
Your heart now weights you down in pain.
The large hole with its very existence,
that you cannot seem to bare its pain,
as you often think about your loss.
Throughout the days that come and go,
thinking of her laughter, those many days ago,
which brings her, that much closer to you.
Your spirit now wants to be connected,
with these very special thoughts of her.
Your healing trowel has now begun,
to smooth away this very pain.
Tears are now bringing her that much closer to you.
Though you cannot touch her body,
your tears have brought her back to you.
Lock these thoughts in your memory,
to aid you with life's ups and downs.
Her body is gone; but not her memory
No good-byes of her remain,
as you wrap her in your mind and memory,
like you have done so many times before.
This simple deed will comfort you,
and your spirit peace, will then have come.

Author: Stephen Paul Tolmie

THINKING OF YOU

My soul is very heavy;
My heart is barely there.
You were my very world.
But no longer are you there.
I am like a burned- out candle.
My life is black and grim.
I truly need you in my life,
to glow this candle again;
to have the warmth of love and light
that only you could show.
I had the world with a glow
as my world was with you.
Now I can only pray to God,
that you will return to me,
my circle of life completed
with you and me entwined
for all eternity.

Author: Stephen Paul Tolmie

MY SPIRIT IS ON HIGH

The touch of your soft warm hand;
Its closeness it brought me to you.
The smile that glowed from your face
I fell more in love with you.
My silent spirit now awakened,
And my heart was all aglow,
As you became a part of my life
And I would never let you go,
We had now been bonded together
As happiness became a part of us.
Love was there for us to share
To pledge our love and life together
To never break this bonded seal.
Your world was now a part of mine.
My world was now with you.
Our body spirits both on high;
Our lives were born renewed.
For now we had found each other
With the true meaning for love and life;
Its pathway set for us to follow
Forever in that direction;
To walk hand and hand forever
Where ever life may lead us,
Whatever strife may greet us
Our love for one another
Will always see us through

Author: Stephen Paul Tolmie

MY LAST THOUHGHTS AS I LEAVE THIS EARTH

As I walk with death, leaving this life behind
Knowing, I have stumbled, through pleasures and strife
I knew not when, my life's journey would end
As living life on earth, is not our end
For time stands still, not even when asked
Though death may be cheated from time to time
But death is not the final end, there is yet more to come
We turn to a spiritual form, when our body's life is finally done
To meet our spiritual leader, and see what HE shall say
It is what we have done between these two times
That truly marks our fate
So fear not as you knock on the eternal door
For it is, as it was, when you were there before
And God's love will hold you ever more
As you are rekindled with loved ones
For eternal life ever more

Author: Stephen Paul Tolmie

PEOPLE COME INTO OUR LIVES; FOR A REASON!

People come into our lives for a reason, a season, or a lifetime. When you know which one it is, you will know what to do; for that person.

When someone is in your life for a REASON, it is usually to meet a need; which you have expressed. They have come to assist you, through a difficulty; to provide you with guidance and support; to aid you physically, emotionally or spiritually.

That may seem like a Godsend, and they are! They are there for the "Reason" you need them to be! Then, without any wrongdoing on your part, or at any inconvenient time; this person will say something; to bring the relationship to an end.

Sometimes they die; sometimes they walk away, and sometimes they force you to take a stand. What we must realize; is that "your need" has been met; your "desire" has been fulfilled. Their work is done! The prayer, you sent; has been answered, and now it is time to move on.

Some people come into your lives, for a SEASON; because your turn has come to share, to grow, or to learn. They bring you an experience, or peace; or make you laugh. They may teach you something you have never done? They usually give you, an unbelievable amount of joy. Believe it! It is real…. but only for a "Season"!

LIFETIME relationships; teach your lifetime lessons; things you must build upon; in order to have a solid emotional foundation. Your job is to accept the lesson; love the person, and put what you have learned to use; in all other relationships, and areas of your life.

It is often said; that "Love is Blind" but "Friendship is Clairvoyant"!

Thank you, for being a part of my life; whether you were there for a REASON, a SEASON, or a LIFETIME!

AN AUTHOR'S THOUGHT
TO THE WISE!

Knowing you, dealing with the issues; handling loss, and the stress in one's life; is important! Looking at the broad picture of death, near death experiences; coming back from death and along with all the other up's and down's; in your life. We have been examining, a whole gambit of life; death, rebirth from handling grief, and knowing what to do in preparing for death. I thought, we should take a short breather; and just examine; the basic lessons we have learned; so in doing this, here are my thoughts.

Years from now, you will have had many disappointments; rejections, bad experiences and sad moments. This all stems, by the actions you didn't take, or possibly by the actions; you did take?

It is now time, to unburden yourself; and start a new path in your life. You will actually walk, that unknown pathway never taken? You will take risk, chances, and been inquisitive; checking out that new horizon.

This can all be a new approach to life, to be adventuresome; to be bold, brave and; willing to take on these new challenges.

Seek the unknown, untested, totally new experiences, new obstacles, and those new unchartered waterways of life!

Move forward, discover, make those new dreams; plant your feet on the first step of uncertainty; and willingly to give it your all!

Enjoy your final years, to be happy within yourself; to be a free spirit, and take pleasure; in all your new accomplishments!

FOOD FOR THOUGHT: Good friends are like rare jewels in life. They are difficult to find, and impossible to replace. We meet for a reason; either you are a BLESSING or a LESSON! I hope, looking at my thoughts to the wise; you will start to look at yourself differently? You may realize, that truly there is; some truth in my statements? You shouldn't be afraid to expose you to others; and reap the benefits, that life may be offering; by taking that chance?

THE THINGS YOU CANNOT RECOVER IN LIFE!

THE STONE............................ After it is thrown, lightly or hard,

the effect is still felt. DAMAGE!

THE WORD.............................. After it is spoken,

You await its effect. UNKNOWN!

THE OCCASION .... After it has been enjoyed;

or been missed. THE RESULTS!

THE TIME...................................... After it is gone, it reminds you,

How precious it was. REALITY!

THE PERSON .... After they die, they are only

left in your memory. LEGACY!

My best friend, soulmate, and my confidant; was my wife. She always had my best interest in her heart, as well as on her mind. She always had my back, and was my rock; refuse, and shield from life's problems.

She was my healer, my safe harbour; and my anchor in life!

I wrote a poem, especially in her honour; as a tribute. To reflect, all she was in my life's journey; on the calm and rough seas of life. How she was always there, and now what is left; is such a large void. This now occupies, what was HER place; with the life I am now living.

YOU ALWAYS PULLED
ME THROUGH

When life throws me a little curve
and puts me down each time;
you became my rock and strength
as you always pulled me through.

When I am both down and out,
you put your arms around me
and chased away my blues
as you always pulled me through.

When the weather was cold and grey
your warm smile and kind words
then made the world renewed
as you always pulled me through.

When I needed a warm embrace
you're always there each time;
to let me know how much I'm loved
as you always pulled me through.

You were my balance to life's unknowns
with thoughts of holding you in my arms,
my very needs were then complete.
as you always pulled me through.

Now, at last you have discovered
your love is but a few tears away
as now your my Special Angel

who watches from above
as you always pull me through

from that day forth and ever on.......

to last for all eternity.

Author: Stephen Paul Tolmie

I have stated, in the very beginning of this book; that I was a firm believer, in the fact that you are given a NUMBER; when you were born. This number, you carry all through your life; from your birth till your death. I also believe, in the existence of God and Heaven; and would like to put this message forward. The reason, I feel as I do; and how it affects my attitude; my inner feelings; and about life as a whole. These are the reason, why I don't fear death; and the afterlife to come.

I had attended church in my earlier teen years, and had heard many a sermons; and actually felt that I wanted to become a minister. Believe it or not? I actually gave a sermon in church, yes just one; but I did experience, closeness to God. In my young adult life, I slowly drifted away from going to church. However, my personal beliefs were still intact; and my love for God; still very present in my life.

I wasn't getting much from the sermons, and honestly felt that I didn't need to go to a building; to be close to God. I could be close to God, whenever I wanted to pray.

To put this in my personal perspective; I have made meals, been out for meals, being to friends for meals, but for the life of me; I can't remember a single one? The one, I made for myself last night; as the only exception to this rule. This isn't to say, that those meals didn't give me nourishment; and the strength to do my work or tasks. I completed, all that were laid out for me to accomplish. In fact, if I hadn't had any meals in a long period of time; I likely would be dead!

In the same vein of thought; had I not kept the Holy Spirit, God, and the Resurrection of my body/soul in the foreground of my mind; I wouldn't have the spiritual nourishment; which kept me aware of His Divine Power. In fact, had I not; had this nourishment, I wouldn't know of HIS Promise for Ever Lasting Life; which I value in my everyday life!

So, when someone says of me; why I'm a believer in God and the After Life, this is the parable; that I tell them. I find it an easy, and understandable way; of connecting my faith and beliefs. This leaves the unbeliever, then to look; at the logic and common sense of my statements. He/she then has to come up with his/her own understanding, to formulate his/her own opinion; on the subject.

When you are DOWN to NOTHING; GOD is UP to SOMETHING!

FAITH sees the INVISIBLE, BELIEVES the INCREDIBLE; and RECEIVES the IMPOSSIBLE!!

IF YOU CANNOT SEE GOD IN ALL YOU CANNOT SEE GOD AT ALL!!!

The very interpretation of the word................. B. I. B. L. E.

BASIC INSTRUCTIONS BEFORE LEAVING EARTH!!!

I now feel, we have come to the full circle; of our exploration of near death experiences, experiencing death and returning. We have, also looked at after death; and the next life of been with God in Heaven. I would now, like to add my closing thoughts; at this point in my book. Some of this is WILL BE A REPEAT! My soul purpose is to leave you with a TOTAL IMPACT! I hope, that all the previous material; which has been written for you to digest, will possibly allow you; to reflect on it? It may cause you to see, how it applies or not; to your personal life, and even your thought process?

When you lose a loved one; there has to be a total re-adjustment in life styles, and life's little habits. There is a distinct loss, a void of emptiness; loneliness sets in, and a total new life; for you, to create for yourself.

Everything is Gone! The life preserver, you had when you were flailing in the sea of life; is now gone. Your comfort zone is empty, there are no loving arms to hold you; and give you a sense of security; and peace in your time of pain. You are totally "ON YOUR OWN and FEELING LOST"!

You now question your every decision, your strength of conviction; and your very purpose in life. Everything, now seems like it happened so long ago! You now feel like a new born baby....feeling helpless, needing direction, support and a gentle shove; to take those first steps. Fear and uncertainty, are always present; and you are ever mindful; of the existing "NEW LIFE……………….. ALONE"!

I AM ALONE

I AM SCARED

I AM UNHAPPY

I AM UNLOVED

You are not sure, why you are here; or even, if you really want to be here? You are like that ship, floating on the ocean; not sure where the currents are taking you?

Now, I ask you to look at YOUR LIFE……Where is it Now? You need to take stock in what direction you wish to go? I don't doubt that the walls of uncertainty have started to build up around you? They probably, make you feel almost claustrophobic?

How do you bring these walls down? How do you find the ability, to take the first step; which is the beginning, into the unknown and untested zone; of uncertainty? To a place, where your life will take on a whole new meaning—a new expression of "YOU" and not "US" any longer?

Well......"Come on Down"....and lets build you a new life—a new Comfort Zone. A place, where you now discover yourself; your desires, and your plans for the future, your very purpose; in this thing called "LIFE"!

In this new life, you will have absolutely no control of its impact on your feelings, your thoughts, what you perceive, and the "correct path" to follow; to achieve your goals. This new life should be more than just "BARE EXISTENCE"! You should aspire, to achieve full contentment; and to live out the rest of your days, with a SENSE of Actually Living Life!

I would now, like to insert some poems; which I wrote, which are close to my heart. Hopefully, it may reflect on most people; when they lose a loved one, which was their soulmate in life? This may cause you to reflect back; on your own emotions at the time. The very thoughts that were in existence and what actually did come to your mind; in your hour of Grief?

MISSING YOU IN MY LIFE

My life is very hollow
and full of deep despair.
I long for you in my life
to make my spirit glow,
as only you can do.

You made my world so content
to function the whole day through.

Now my life is without you.
Life's speed bumps drag me down.

My world is in a downward spiral;
an imminent crash faces me!

For your arms are not there to hold me;
to free me from this fate…..
to turn my world from upside down
to right side up with you!

Author: Stephen Paul Tolmie

IF I COULD ONLY HAVE

If I could only have, a small piece of you,
I'd like a little of your heart;
so I could feel your love at night.

If I could only have, a small piece of you,
I'd like a little of your smile;
to brighten up my day.

If I could only have, a small piece of you,
I'd like a little, of the gleam in your eyes;
to make my day just sparkle
with loving thoughts of you.

If I could only have, a small piece of you,
I'd like a bit of your caring ways
so I could feel close to you

If I could only have, a small piece of you,
in truth, the total you;
for now I know, how lonely life can be.
The shadows follow me, time won't set me free.
But yet, when you're around, my spirit is content

Life is now rich and full
with you now safe in my arms
for all eternity.
My love for you is now and always
and my life is finally complete.

Author: Stephen Paul Tolmie

MY CONNECTION TO YOU

I think that I should never see
a lovelier site than that of thee
My heart carries a stronger beat
with your presence so close to me.

I cherished your look all day through,
making me wanting to be closer to you.
Your very smile, takes me through my day.
As my spirit blends, close with you.

If the good Lord should ever take you,
I would surely like to die
if I cannot hold you in my arms.

Then I would wish to leave this place
as my heart would surely die
Your smile would only be a memory
and your touch a sheer unknown
I would long to unite our spirits
Having once again….you and me
for all eternity.
We would then once again
be able to live, to laugh and love.

A loving connection to one another
as in never ending; but lasting flow
of me to another, through all infinity.

Author: Stephen Paul Tolmie

MY SPECIAL FRIEND

Here lies my teacher.
Here lies my companion in life.
Here lies my friend.
Here lies my loving wife.

I was blessed to have known her
and have her leave her imprint on my life.
She taught me all life's rights and wrongs;
to better see the world, with very open eyes.
For my thought process of this world
was often seen with clouded eyes.

To take a single moment and put things all in focus
often giving fresh meaning, a life being born renewed,
to not make a snap decision, like I often do.
But instead, to take that extra moment
to totally, think things through.

It is truly amazing......
the thinking capacity.
So, now things don't look so grey,
In fact, they are crystal blue.

As I said...she was my teacher;
and now I'm a better man.
The world's a better place
totally because of you!

Author: Stephen Paul Tolmie

HER SMILE AND TOUCH
IS DAILY MISSED

I was thinking of you today

As, I do, affectionately everyday

I think about the things we said and did

As though, it was done just yesterday.

I miss your presence, your touch, your grace;

As my mind, draws me back, to these bygone days.

My heart is touched, my mind now at peace.

I long to be with you, to feel your touch;

For then again, you become a part of me

Rest now my love, my lady

My love will never die.

Someday we'll to be together,

Our spirits joined as one

Locked together, for all eternity

Author: Stephen Paul Tolmie

We have now covered; the whole scheme of life, living life, feeling life, and losing a partner in life, and the life here after; to help cope with one's inner feelings and beliefs. This then, will encourage you to speak with loved ones; family and friends more openly. In keeping, that open mind; not all will be in agreement with you. Possibly, your common sense and logic will prevail; with the final outcome; that each are allowed their opinions. That in itself, is what life is all about; the giving and taking aspect. I hope it helps you, avoid some of the life's pitfalls; which were all too common; in your life time. Hopefully, these pitfalls still can be avoided; in your remaining time, here on earth?

I hope this book; has given you a little bit of inner peace, of comfort and a sense of closeness, to the loved ones; who have gone before you? Now, you have the chance; to look deep within yourself; to see what you have done, and possibly, the time to correct; pass mistakes? Using this time, to re-evaluate; who and what your religious beliefs are? For you to think, what possibly may exist; with God and Heaven above? Now, hopefully, possessing a new outlook on your life; and your personal opinion on the life hereafter?

Is there a Saint Peter at the Pearly Gates; who checks HIS book on your account? Have you PASSED the grade or have you FALLEN short?

As we now struggle, to believe the best is yet to come! We are now, holding dear; the memories of those we loved. As they pass, from this world ahead of us; we try to find comfort in a faith, which is beyond us.

Turning to the Bible, I would like to insert Romans 8; beginning at verse 31, where the Apostle Paul writes:

"What then are we to say about these things? If God is for us, who is against us?" It is in times of sadness and emotional turmoil that the light of God seems the furthest away. It is through pain of human loss, that God carries us, if we allow ourselves to be carried.

Finally, another quotation from the Bible; Palms 121, brings us words of assurance of God's protection:

I lift up my eyes to see the mountains-
where does my help come from?
My help comes from the Lord,
the Maker of heaven and earth.

He will not let your foot slip-
he who watches over you, will not slumber;
indeed, he who watches over Israel
will neither slumber nor sleep.

The Lord watches over you-
The Lord is your shade at your right hand;
The sun will not harm you by day,
nor the moon by night.

The Lord will keep you from all harm-
He watches over your life;
the Lord will watch over, you're coming and going
both now and forever more.

Let us hear the promise of God:

John 11: 25-36 Jesus said: I am the resurrection and the life. Those who believe in me, even though they die will live and everyone who lives and believes in me; shall never die.

Jesus said: "I go to make a place for you".........

My final thoughts as I finish off this book; are to leave you with a poem, I wrote; called "A DAILEY PRAYER." This I feel expresses what a person's outlook on life; is all about. One should be happy, with all the gifts that has been given; to appreciate them; and don't take them for granted.

I think in this prayer, it covers most; if not all aspects, of what a person should be thankful for. I feel in a small way; it does indeed fall under the topic of "WHEN IS YOUR TIME UP"?

It reflects on almost every aspect, of everyone's life. Making you appreciate the time you have had on this earth. Remembering these values in your life, and hopefully; following these standards; when your NUMBER is finally up. I hope that it shows, that you left your mark; you're imprint on this earth; and that your memory will get carried on, for all to remember you; and your time on earth!

As in the final message, in my poem; it brings the point home:

"MUCH IS GIVEN IN LIFE; AND MUCH IS REQUIRED OF US IN LIFE".

"LIVE FOR THE MOMENTS…YOU CAN'T PUT INTO WORDS"

A DAILEY PRAYER

I am thankful for the gift of life.

I am thankful for the ability to love.

I am thankful for each new day.

I am thankful for laughter and song.

I am thankful for compassion.

I am thankful for family and friends.

I am thankful for a smile.

I am thankful for our wisdom.

I am thankful for our courage.

I am thankful for our strength,
that comes from within when needed.

May all our thanks be present each day?
as much is given to us in life;
and much is required, by us in return.

AMEN

Author: Stephen Paul Tolmie

ABOUT THE AUTHOR

I was born in a small town of St. Thomas, Ontario, Canada and lived there for the first twenty years of my life; before moving to London.

As in all small towns, everyone knows everyone else's business and their secrets. There is no end to gossip and rumours to spread around. This can aid a writer in some good writing material, if he /she wish to incorporate it; into their writing.

I worked for the Provincial government for thirty years, and retired at the ripe old age of fifty; (50) as per the government eighty point system................age plus years of service.

Not knowing what to do with myself, with "free time" now on my hands; I felt lost? I volunteered at a nursing/retirement home for a year, but found that they demanded too much of my time; on a weekly basis. Although, I liked the people I dealt with; management was abusing my good intentions.

I then found a hobby job, I thought initially; working as a parking lot attendant, at a local school; known as Fanshawe College in London, ON. I worked there for ten additional years, (now a job & not a hobby); as I enjoyed speaking with the variety of people, both staff and students. I didn't like the early hours, or the standing out in all kinds of weather; to complete this job. Also, another drawback; was paying additional income tax, on this hobby money. I was paying most of my money in earnings, to the government. NOT TOO BRIGHT ON MY PART!!!

The phrase comes to mind: "AS BRIGHT AS A 10 WATT BULB"?

I decided, I would; like a new venture in my life's journey, and decided to write. This had always been on my bucket list, of things I wanted to try to do; in my life time, before I meet my Maker!

Here is a list, of some of the books I have written; for you to check out, if you have the inclination; and the web site is at: www.authorhouse.com OR Phone Number 1 (800) 839-8640

Now You Have Her…..Now You Don't

My attempt in writing this book; was also an attempt to heal myself; in my emotional time of Grief. God knows, I am qualified to write this; as I have experienced the loss of my wife, to cancer in 2004. In writing this book, it has given me the knowledge; to try and assist others; to move forward in their lives. Your love for your spouse is forever, and your thoughts will always keep them; in a special place in your heart.

That Single Moment

This book, deals with the emotions of losing a loved one; and with the healing process, which one goes through; to "restart" a personal life. I have attempted in this book, to create a "fictional character" (which is actually me); who deals with what I call, the four "C's" of Grief.

Connecting to Grief
Coping with Grief
Conquering Grief
Continuing Life without Grief

In using these, four elements in my story line; shows this fictional character; working his way through this process.

Estate Planning & Executor Guide

In writing this book, I am attempting (as a non-professional) to assist people. Using my personal knowledge, and research materials; into this very subject, of what is involved. In an attempt, to describe what it actually means; and the numerous processes; you have to be aware of and execute. This book could help you, in setting up; your own Estate Planning! It also helps, make your aware of the responsibilities; and commitment, prior to accepting the position; of becoming an executor.

THE QUEST

In writing this book, it was an attempt to look inward; to try and understand; what makes me, who I am. Using the 5 W's (why, when, where, who and what) as an examination of my actions, and my need to perform. Not always in a good format, in my younger years; and why I felt, I needed to do what I did; in the situations that occurred.

In later years, it was an attempt to understand the "How's" and the "Why's" and the "Wherefores" about the person in this body. Why were all these emotions, or lack of emotions; needed to express my pain and my anxiety? Why was I not following through, with what my brain was saying? Why would my heart, not allow the proper actions to be put in place; with the situation at hand?

LIFE.........LUST........LOVE

In this background setting, I took my life's experiences for this book. I have tried to enlighten the reader, about how "inept" I was; in pursuing someone special in my life. I am not trying to appear as the victim; but rather as someone, who was struggling to follow in the footsteps; of those who had the life skills. Somehow, I seemed to be totally lacking, and completely out of my element; in my quest for a partner in life.

My utopia was to find someone special, going together through life's ups and downs; and build some very special memories.

SMILES POEMS....THOUGHTS TO PONDER

In writing this book, it too was on my bucket list; to attempt writing some poetry. Were even possible? I did however succeed! This book also contains in the beginning, some humorous comments and some great thoughts. Also, statements made by a variety of well-known statesmen's, philosophers and other notables; thought provoking!

"WHEN IS YOUR TIME UP"?

This book examines many aspects of; near death experiences, coming back from death, grieving death of a loved one and preparation for death. It also helps you, in understanding how to organize your Personal Estate. Also, it covers having an executor of your estate; just to mention a few of the topics, under review.

We first should examine what our lives involve, what happens in our lives; and what are our expectations; with our death? Also, the effects of our death on people; left behind with our death. What is the outcome of our death on them? How it did affect them with our death?

We are here for really a very short period of time, and we have no knowledge; of when that time period will be up? Be it for a long or short period of years? We have gathered our wealth, tried to look after our health; but really, the important thing in our lives; is our SPIRIT. What will become of it? Unfortunately, we spend very little of our precious time; even contemplating, the hereafter, and what is to become; of our SPIRIT SOULS.

Printed in the United States
By Bookmasters